• THE BARNES & NOBLE LIBRARY OF ESSENTIAL READING •

CONVERSATIONS WITH SOCRATES

Xenophon

Translated by Edward Bysshe

Introduction by Odysseus Makridis

BARNES & NOBLE

NEW YORK

THE BARNES & NOBLE
LIBRARY OF ESSENTIAL READING

Cover Design by Stacey May

2005 Barnes & Noble Publishing, Inc.

ISBN 0-7607-7044-1

Printed and bound in the United States of America

1 3 5 7 9 10 8 6 4 2

CONTENTS

INTRODUCTION

SOCRATES was not the first philosopher in the Western tradition but he was certainly the first known to have lived a life fully devoted to thinking. Socrates himself did not write anything down. The writings of two of his followers, Plato and Xenophon, have reached posterity and preserved for us a portrait of the great philosopher. While Plato's depiction of Socrates is refracted through the author's sophisticated preoccupations and philosophical doctrines, Xenophon's Socrates is lively and behaves, discourses, admonishes, and counsels in ways in which even the non-specialist reader will find impressive, memorable, and greatly useful. Xenophon's immediate purpose in this work is to vindicate Socrates and defend his tarnished reputation; but his ultimate purpose arches over the aeons to bring Socrates to us, engaging and irresistible, animated by irrefutable common sense, a sagacious and pragmatic advisor correcting our faltering steps and making life's ordeals bearable.

Socrates (469–399 BCE) was the obscure son of a statue maker, not destined for greatness in the strictly hierarchical society of Athens. But his magnetic personality, keen intellect, and devotion to the "examined life" ensured his place in history. Socrates had a mission, not simply a transitory interest in the creative use of the intellect. His mission apparently was to seek the truth about the perennial and most engaging human questions. His method was to ask questions, demand that concepts be clearly defined, and attempt to refute the replies given to him—not in order to embarrass, although he did that too incidentally, but under the assumption that anything that can be refuted cannot be the truth. His impact was mainly negative and critical but it does not follow from this that his mood or views were skeptical. Socrates was informed by a deep and abiding optimism: that ultimate and coherent answers to the deepest questions exist, that truth and moral goodness are related and ensured by the fabric of the universe, and that the morally best and happiest life is the life of philosophical inquiry, even if such inquiry does not reap the rewards of specific and articulate discoveries.

The fame of Socrates owes also a good deal to the manner of his death. Charged with impiety and corruption of the young, he was found guilty of the charges. Rather than accept his wealthy friends' advice to bribe the guards and secure his escape, he bravely swallowed a poison, hemlock, and died. Plato claims that Socrates was still discoursing and trying to prove the immortality of the soul to his grieving friends on the day of his death. Socrates is also supposed to have discussed and refuted his friends' suggestion that civil disobedience, and escape from prison and death, were justified under the circumstances. Socrates' imperturbability and moral mettle are in evidence in the anecdote preserved about the moment of his death: With his last words Socrates asked his friends to give Asclepius, the god of health, a votive offering that he had promised on a previous occasion.

Socrates has had his detractors. His strict rationalism, objectivist position on the problem of truth, and moral certainty have not been in favor among contemporary philosophers like Nietzsche and his various students. By the same token, Socrates offers one of the most potent antidotes for any era to pervasive skepticism, moral relativism, and irrationalist experimentation.

The present volume, rendered as *Conversations with Socrates*, is a translation of Xenophon's work *Sokratous Apomnemoneumata*, which can, and has been, translated also as *The Memorabilia of Socrates*. Xenophon was motivated by the task of restoring Socrates' reputation and this might have interfered with his reconstruction of what

Socrates said and did not say. It is also arguable that Xenophon might have failed to fully follow Socrates in his more soaring philosophical flights. Nevertheless, we cannot completely rule out the possibility that Socrates might have been more like Xenophon's down-to-earth advisor rather than Plato's complex thinker.

Conversations with Socrates is presented as a most detailed defense of Socrates. Like Plato, Xenophon also wrote a *Speech of Defense* echoing the presumably impromptu oration that Socrates had delivered in front of an Athenian jury in the famous trial that sealed the philosopher's fate and inflicted enduring shame on Athenian democracy. Unlike Plato, whom he accused of making Socrates sound too arrogant in his defense, Xenophon went on to elaborate further on the rebuttal of the charges against Socrates. *Conversations with Socrates* is meant as this elaboration. This is not a longer speech but a reflection of Socrates' life — the true and most irrefutable defense. Since conversations with others were the essential, most cherished, and defining elements of Socrates' life, Xenophon's book teems with exchanges between the revered guru Socrates and various Athenians. Unlike Plato's Socrates, Xenophon's Socrates addresses both famous and obscure citizens and offers advice that ranges from persuasive marshaling of arguments to practical how-to, nuts-and-bolts instructions. This suggests that Socrates was not an anti-democratic elitist after all, in spite of what the average Athenian might have gathered from seeing Socrates whispering impressively over admiring aristocratic youths, many of whom went on to pursue demagogic careers and cast blight and ruin on Athens. It must be pointed out, however, that even Xenophon, who will not heap Plato's invectives on democracy, tends to avoid this subject and simply rests content with presenting a non-condescending Socrates, friend to every man — a Socrates, moreover, who once stood up to tyrants fearlessly and castigated them for their violent desires and pathological injustice.

The book is framed soberly, often tenderly, with Xenophon's persistent pleading: Socrates was innocent of the malicious charges of which he was, alas, eventually found guilty. Xenophon insists, and seeks to prove beyond doubt, that Socrates was pious and a sturdy moral teacher who benefited his associates with both his words and his example. This book might be the first biography in the Western tradition. Interestingly enough, this first biography has the twin purposes of showing a just man for who he truly was, and of setting the record straight by deploying a whole lifetime of conversations and ideas that go beyond the narrow confines of the due process that proved ruinous for Socrates. The first biography was intended as a record of a hidden truth, not a self-deconstructing or free-flowing exercise in creativity.

Since the objective of the work is to vindicate Socrates' memory, it is reasonable to wonder whether it speaks the truth. We cannot give a definitive answer to this question. We can refer to Xenophon's credentials, recorded life experiences, and apparent features of character. The reader may make up his or her own mind. To be fair, passing judgment on Xenophon is not an easy task as there are both appealing and disagreeable aspects to what we know about him. Xenophon (444–c. 357 BCE) was apparently a good soldier, even elected to the rank of general, an adventurer in the style of later self-aggrandizing conquerors of faraway lands. He recorded his exploits but did so with a view to addressing the broader contours of historical events and his capacities in this respect are not altogether meager: though not a profound thinker, Xenophon clearly possessed ample common sense, political shrewdness, practical acumen, a quick intelligence, a pleasant urbanity, and a capacity to pay attention to details that are consistent with his narrative. His temperament was conservative and indeed pro-Spartan: he preferred the militaristic, disciplined, culturally backward, deliberately anti-intellectualist, and anti-progressive Spartan regime to Athenian openness, progressive eclecticism, and cultural experimentation. His writing, however, is not boorish, propagandistic, polemical, or predictable. Students of applied disciplines might actually find him a good deal more relevant than Plato. Most cursory readers would take him to be objective. His preferences peep through occasionally, as, for instance, when he has Socrates frequently lament the present state of "decadent" Athens and express a decided preference for Spartan institutions, way of life, and even specific military tactics.

Xenophon liked to write and his writing is lucid, informative, alive with practical intelligence, and surprisingly vibrant with between-the-lines meanings. He is not disingenuous or unctuous in his praise of, and claims to, certain virtues; at the same time, his career demonstrated a lack of a virtue such as patriotism, which one would have demanded of someone of his ilk and ideology. This is not necessarily an instance of contradiction or hypocrisy. Like Machiavelli—who may have patterned his *Prince* consciously in relation to certain Xenophontic mirrors or princes—Xenophon might have appreciated the inexorable operation of higher-level moral dilemmas which greatly complicate theories of goodness. Like Machiavelli, Xenophon eschews philosophical speculation, and his shrewd astuteness can be discerned only when the reader is willing to take the author seriously. It is therefore intriguing that such a writer would have set himself the goal of saving Socrates' reputation. Xenophon's fondness for Socrates appears to be sincere and unadorned. His indignation over the fate of Socrates is genuine. Xenophon might have taken the condemnation of Socrates as one more sign of Athenian degeneration. And, it seems, Xenophon found in Socrates something precious and meaning-bestowing—a common reaction, apparently, for all those who met and came under the spell of Socrates.

In *Conversations with Socrates*, Xenophon operates like a skilled attorney or a specialist hired to clear one's reputation by means of a carefully coordinated media campaign. Xenophon's Socrates does not speak from above nor reduce his interlocutors to numbness and confusion, as Plato's Socrates so often does. Xenophon's Socrates cannot be taken for a fearsome personality—not even for an enigmatic one. In writing about Socrates, Xenophon is a sincere, earnest, skilled, pragmatic campaigner who works hard to persuade without violating truth impermissibly and without stooping to popular imbecility. He does not compromise his moral convictions which, moreover, he might genuinely believe to be consistent with those of Socrates himself.

While the more profound Plato's moral indignation stems partly from a pessimistic, even misanthropic, assessment of human nature, the more pedestrian and optimistic Xenophon trusts the average person's good faith, common sense, and ultimate susceptibility to proof and reasoning. *Conversations with Socrates* is based on this premise. Plato would not have thought it sensible, or even potentially effective, to write a defense of Socrates along the lines pursued by Xenophon. But even Plato, at least in what are presumed to be his earlier works, goes through the motions of using Socratic conversations to refute vulgar misperceptions and malicious rumors about the historical Socrates. Of course, Xenophon can never be confused with Plato in a most important respect: unlike Plato, Xenophon is immune to the seduction of philosophical speculation. Even so, Xenophon succeeds in attributing to Socrates a remarkably coherent viewpoint, which remains consistent and is argued throughout the work. Xenophon himself seems to subscribe to this viewpoint wholeheartedly. This Socratic viewpoint is unexpectedly pragmatic, concrete, and prudential. It is not unexpected that Socrates would be cautioning and exhorting to self-control, moderation in public affairs, and related virtues. What is surprising is that Xenophon's Socrates places prudence above even the search for truth — or, at least, so it seems. Of course, there might be a deeper meaning: that one must appear quiescent to preserve one's life; and, certainly, one must remain alive if one wishes to continue to philosophize — although the more mystically inclined Plato would doubt this.

Those who are familiar with Plato's Socrates might find the Socrates of the *Conversations* to be rather unphilosophical. If Plato's Socrates sounds like one of those professors whose class you failed in college, Xenophon's Socrates is the next-door neighbor whose advice you always avidly seek out — from how to make and keep friends, treat your teenage children, survive in times of economic downturn, to how to be in good standing with the local sheriff and handle unruly, pestering relatives. This homespun aspect of Socrates is not altogether missing from Plato's writings, but in Xenophon it seems to have absorbed almost everything else. A theory is presented, mantra-like: be smart enough to understand that doing the right thing will keep you out of trouble and might even yield benefits.

The shock of discovering a discrepancy between the Platonic and the Xenophontic Socrates is mitigated somewhat when we look more closely at Xenophon's work. Then we can detect many a Socratic preoccupation with which we are familiar from Plato's works: the famous question-answer-refutation-reformulation method, hostility to empty rhetoric, emphasis on moral subjects, rejection of natural philosophy, insistence that terms be defined clearly and thoughtfully, and reasoned support for moralizing conclusions. We also detect the Platonic view that moral exhortation is the prime task of a thinker, confidence that reason is the authority in moral deliberation, promotion of temperance in relation to bodily desires, withering criticisms of irrational popular opinions, ample use of analogies from especially the practices of menial vocations and the skills needed for navigation, a healthy appetite for puns and jokes, and Socrates' celebrated fearlessness in the presence of powerful people and even in response to menacing bullying.

Several features and habits of the Platonic Socrates, however, are missing from Xenophon's narration: Xenophon's Socrates is not as irksomely ironic as Plato's; he does not reduce his fellow discussants—especially the self-important ones—to shambles; he does not vaunt his rhetorical prowess; he is not interested in philosophizing for the sake of philosophizing or in abstract and speculative questions about the nature of things; he is not interested in the magical, potentially dangerous, seductive potency of Eros (Xenophon's Socrates is not an erotic mystery, at once both ugly and alluring, as Plato's is, but he is instead an old man who, literally, offers to serve as procurer for a concubine rather than have youths fall in love with him.) Xenophon's Socrates treats argument, dialectic, as he treats rhetoric itself, as mere instruments for the promotion of objectives that are healthy and good in themselves. He does not use philosophy as an end in itself and does not regard philosophizing as the authoritative eye that can peer into the nature of reality. Perhaps Xenophon's hint is that Socrates courted danger by gaining the reputation of one who lived and cherished the philosophic life. Of course, Plato is not at all embarrassed by this reputation of Socrates and elevated the martyred thinker onto a pedestal on which posterity has taken stock of him. Xenophon's Socrates is more of an unassuming and helpful wise old neighbor and occasionally brave citizen; he is not a controversial icon or martyr.

It is reasonable that Xenophon might have omitted aspects of Socrates that could attract bad publicity: Socrates' formidable intellectualism, his erotic magnetism, his puzzling speculative tangents — these were mesmerizing facets of the Socrates legend which backfired and cost Socrates his life. Charismatic demagogues, like Alcibiades, were attracted to Socrates; later, they won elections and led Athens to catastrophe. Xenophon handles this subject by claiming that such types had behaved well, under the influence of Socrates' speeches and moral example, for as long as they were his followers. They deteriorated and turned calamitous after they were no longer with Socrates.

Xenophon asks the philosophically interesting question as to whether moral impressions can indeed prove ephemeral—which is not necessarily consistent with the Socratic dictum, known to Xenophon, that moral excellence is identical with knowledge. It is unlikely that one would have forgotten the old teacher's words and example so easily. Characteristically, Xenophon does not pursue the philosophical question but does something that is both prudent and pragmatic at the same time: he adds another dimension to the moral equation. Perhaps people like Alcibiades are incorrigible after all; this is evidenced by the fact that Alcibiades persisted for a while in following Socrates for the wrong reasons: to learn how to be a self-promoting, formidable orator. Apparently,

Alcibiades did not learn, and continued to pay attention to the form rather than the content of Socrates' teachings. This, however, can also redound against Socrates, and Xenophon knows it. Indeed, if there is something dangerous about the form or rhetoric of Socratic persuasion, this might be a sufficient reason to consider Socrates an unwelcome member of a community. Xenophon parries this challenge with characteristic dexterity—a skill that the casual reader can easily miss. According to Xenophon, when Alcibiades was still under the spell of Socrates, he did occasionally check and question the hypocrisy of authority. Alcibiades' uncle and legal guardian was none other than the legendary statesman Pericles himself. In a brief conversation—the only one without Socrates as a participant—Alcibiades exposes Pericles as a hypocrite, in a subtle way. Perhaps even the very method and technique of Socratic cross-examination suffices to spread a healthy message about justice and good morals.

If there is one inexpugnable irritating facet of this book it must be this: Most of the arguments presented by Socrates return to a basic formula, which we can call a prudential argument. Here is what a prudential argument looks like, to put it simply: you should certainly do X if it is true that doing X will allow you to reap benefits for yourself, at comparatively low cost, now or in the future. Xenophon's Socrates is fond of this line of thinking. This is different from claiming that a *side effect* of doing the right thing may be personal benefit. In prudential reasoning, the expected benefit to oneself is claimed as the main and relevant ethical motivator. Sometimes the confusion behind this has to do with the dual meaning of words like "should" and "ought," which can be rendered both as "you should morally do X" and "if you want to achieve Y, you should instrumentally do X." This was true of Xenophon's Greek as it is of our language.

Xenophon's prudential formula is even more surprising, and possibly a blunder, because the Athenians knew this as a Sophist argument. The Sophists were itinerant teachers of rhetoric and persuasion who catered to the needs of wealthy and ambitious boys. As evidenced by his disastrous trial, Socrates was considered a Sophist by the Athenian public. Plato spent considerable effort in showing that this was a tragic mistake: in fact, Socrates had been arguing against the Sophists and was at cross purposes with them on the account of his elevated unselfish moral teachings. Xenophon would hardly have wished to create the impression that Socrates is a sophistic teacher.

One possible explanation for Xenophon's predilection for attributing a ubiquitous prudential formula to Socrates is this: Xenophon might be trying to have Socrates clinching his moral exhortations with an appeal to personal interest. Xenophon is eager to show not only that Socrates offered the right kind of advice but that Socrates was highly practical and effective. Xenophon may have thought that most people are likely to be persuaded in moral matters only when they come to believe that it is in their interest to do or not to do something.

The reader would certainly want to know if Xenophon succeeds in rebutting the charges against Socrates. But this is something the reader will have to decide. There were, as we recall, two charges against Socrates, and Xenophon attempts to respond to both. Xenophon replies to the charges in the opening of the book and appends, as it were, the anecdotes and conversations with Socrates to reinforce the case he made in the beginning in support of Socrates. Critical readers may discover interesting silences, telltale repetitions, and allusive references throughout the book. For instance, Xenophon does not discuss whether Socrates sacrificed to the gods not only in public but also in private. Xenophon presents Socrates castigating those who seek divination about natural matters but Socrates himself also forbids rational investigation into the nature of things. Xenophon also equivocates as to whether Socrates had any positive teachings or simply taught by example of good character and by addressing specific everyday problems. These and other subtleties can occupy inquisitive readers but it is also the case that the line of reasoning Xenophon deploys is explicitly straightforward and tight.

Regarding the impiety charges, Xenophon insists that Socrates never omitted any practices and rituals that were expected of a good Athenian; Socrates performed ritual services in full view of everyone and in public; Socrates believed in his own personal demon, which indicates that Socrates believed in the existence of demons and, therefore, in the existence of gods who are demons' parents; Socrates even offered advice based on his own divine voice (in Plato, Socrates' voice only causes him to refrain from doing something, never urges him to undertake an initiative); Socrates also taught people to fear the gods because he remonstrated with them to the effect that the gods know even secret and hidden thoughts; Socrates was interested in defining piety with a view to cultivating the virtue of piety; Socrates even went as far as to delineate the specific areas on which divination is or is not to be sought; Socrates always chastised the impious and urged everyone to respect the gods.

Regarding the corruption charge: Socrates always admonished sternly against lack of self-control and extolled the benefits of moderation; he set a wonderful example by shunning excesses in all matters pertaining to bodily desires and in cultivating the pure pleasures of the mind; as someone who was a good and just man himself, he could not have led others to injustice or wickedness; he did not profess to teach anything, and therefore he did not allure litigious and demagogic characters but he taught rather through his good-natured openness and the example he set; he corrected every type of deviant behavior imaginable (and Xenophon is nothing if not detailed in recounting conversations in which Socrates addresses and seeks to rectify nearly every imaginable problem facing people of various stations in life, professions, and characters); Socrates' legendary fearlessness and endurance were an inspiration to all; he never charged money but made his advice available to all those who solicited it, having nothing to hide or hold back.

Xenophon joins the other companions of Socrates who apparently mourned the teacher's death. Xenophon was not in Athens at the time of Socrates' trial and death but this hardly mitigated the passion with which he must have reacted to the ill tidings — the most just man who ever lived had been found guilty of unspeakable, unjust charges and sentenced to death.

Odysseus Makridis received his Ph.D. from Brandeis University. He is Assistant Professor of Philosophy at Fairleigh Dickinson University, in Madison, New Jersey.

BOOK I

CHAPTER I

SOCRATES NOT A CONTEMNER OF THE GODS OF HIS COUNTRY, NOR AN INTRODUCER OF NEW ONES

I have often wondered by what show of argument the accusers of Socrates could persuade the Athenians he had forfeited his life to the State. For though the crimes laid unto his charge were indeed great—"That he did not acknowledge the gods of the Republic; that he introduced new ones"—and, farther, "had debauched the youth;" yet none of these could, in the least, be proved against him."

For, as to the first, "That he did not worship the deities which the Republic adored," how could this be made out against him, since, instead of paying no homage to the gods of his country, he was frequently seen to assist in sacrificing to them, both in his own family and in the public temples?—perpetually worshipping them in the most public, solemn, and religious manner.

What, in my opinion, gave his accusers a specious pretext for alleging against him that he introduced new deities was this—that he had frequently declared in public he had received counsel from a *divine voice,* which he called his Demon. But this was no proof at all of the matter. All that Socrates advanced about his demon was no more than what is daily advanced by those who believe in and practise divination; and if Socrates, because he said he received intelligence from his genius, must be accused of introducing new divinities, so also must they; for is it not certain that those who believe in divination, and practise that belief, do observe the flight of birds, consult the entrails of victims, and remark even unexpected words and accidental occurrences? But they do not, therefore, believe that either the birds whose flight they observe or the persons they meet accidentally know either their good or ill fortune—neither did Socrates—they only believe that the gods make use of these things to presage the future; and such, too, was the belief of Socrates. The vulgar, indeed, imagine it to be the very birds and things which present themselves to them that excite them to what is good for them, or make them avoid what may hurt them; but, as for Socrates, he freely owned that a demon was his monitor; and he frequently told his friends before-hand what they should do, or not do, according to the instructions he had received from his demon; and they who believed him, and followed his advice, always found advantage by it; as, on the contrary, they who neglected his admonitions, never failed to repent their incredulity. Now, it cannot be denied but that he ought to have taken care not to pass with his friends either for a liar or a visionary; and yet how could he avoid incurring that censure if the events had not justified the truth of the things he pretended were revealed to him? It is, therefore, manifest that he would not have spoken of things to come if he had not believed he said true; but how could he believe he said true, unless he believed that the gods, who alone ought to be trusted for the knowledge of things to come, gave him notice of them? and, if he believed they did so, how can it be said that he acknowledged no gods?

He likewise advised his friends to do, in the best manner they could, the things that of necessity they were to do; but, as to those whose events were doubtful, he sent them to the oracles to know whether they should engage in them or not. And he thought that they who design to govern with success their families or whole cities had great need of receiving instructions by the help of divinations; for though he indeed held that every man may make choice of the condition of life in which he desires to live, and that, by his industry, he may render himself excellent in it, whether he apply himself to architecture or to agriculture, whether he throw himself into politics or economy, whether he engage himself in the public revenues or in the army, yet that in all these things the gods have reserved to themselves the most important events, into which men of themselves can in no wise penetrate. Thus he who makes a fine plantation of trees, knows not who shall gather the fruit; he who builds a house cannot tell who shall inhabit it; a general is not certain that he shall be successful in his command, nor a Minister of State in his ministry; he who marries a beautiful woman in hopes of being happy with her knows not but that even she herself may be the cause of all his uneasinesses; and he who enters into a grand alliance is uncertain whether they with whom he allies himself will not at length be the cause of his ruin. This made him frequently say that it is a great folly to imagine there is not a Divine Providence that presides over these things, and that they can in the least depend on human prudence. He likewise held it to be a weakness to importune the gods with questions which we may resolve ourselves; as if we should ask them whether it be better to take a coachman who knows how to drive than one who knows nothing of the matter? whether it be more eligible to take an experienced pilot than one that is ignorant? In a word, he counted it a kind of impiety to consult the oracles concerning what might be numbered or weighed, because we ought to learn the things which the gods have been pleased to capacitate us to know; but that we ought to have recourse to the oracles to be instructed in those that surpass our knowledge, because the gods are wont to discover them to such men as have rendered them propitious to themselves.

Socrates stayed seldom at home. In the morning he went to the places appointed for walking and public exercises. He never failed to be at the hall, or courts of justice, at the usual hour of assembling there, and the rest of the day he was at the places where the greatest companies generally met. There it was that he discoursed for the most part, and whoever would hear him easily might; and yet no man ever observed the least impiety either in his actions or his words. Nor did he amuse himself to reason of the secrets of nature, or to search into the manner of the creation of what the sophists call the world, nor to dive into the cause of the motions of the celestial bodies. On the contrary, he exposed the folly of such as give themselves up to these contemplations; and he asked whether it was, after having acquired a perfect knowledge of human things, that they undertook to search into the divine, or if they thought themselves very wise in neglecting what concerned them to employ themselves in things above them? He was astonished likewise that they did not see it was impossible for men to comprehend anything of all those wonders, seeing they who have the reputation of being most knowing in them are of quite different opinions, and can agree no better than so many fools and madmen; for as some of these are not afraid of the most dangerous and frightful accidents, while others are in dread of what is not to be feared, so, too, among those philosophers, some are of opinion that there is no action but what may be done in public, nor word that may not freely be spoken before the whole world, while others, on the contrary, believe that we ought to avoid the conversation of men and keep in a perpetual solitude. Some have despised the temples and the altars, and have taught not to honour the gods, while others have been so superstitious as to worship wood, stones, and irrational creatures. And as to the knowledge of natural things, some have confessed but one only being; others have admitted an infinite number: some have believed that all things are in a perpetual motion; others that nothing moves: some have held the world to be full of continual generations and corruptions; others maintain that nothing is engendered or destroyed. He said besides that he should be glad to know of those persons whether they were in hopes one day to put in practice what they learned, as men who know an art may practise it when they please either for their own advantage or for the service of their friends; or whether they did imagine that, after they found out the causes of all things that happen, they should be able to cause winds and rains, and to dispose the times and seasons as they had occasion for them; or whether they contented themselves with the bare knowledge without expecting any farther advantage.

This was what he said of those who delight in such studies. As for his part, he meditated chiefly on what is useful and proper for man, and took delight to argue of piety and impiety, of honesty and dishonesty, of justice and injustice, of wisdom and folly, of courage and cowardice, of the State, and of the qualifications of a Minister of State, of the Government, and of those who are fit to govern; in short, he enlarged on the like subjects, which it becomes men of condition to know, and of which none but slaves should be ignorant.

It is not strange, perhaps, that the judges of Socrates mistook his opinion in things concerning which he did not explain himself; but I am surprised that they did not reflect on what he had said and done in the face of the whole world; for when he was one of the Senate, and had taken the usual oath exactly to observe the laws, being in his turn vested with the dignity of Epistate, he bravely withstood the populace, who, against all manner of reason, demanded that the nine captains, two of whom were Erasinides and Thrasilus, should be put to death, he would never give consent to this injustice, and was not daunted at the rage of the people, nor at the menaces of the men in power, choosing rather not to violate the oath he had taken than to yield to the violence of the multitude, and shelter himself from the vengeance of those who threatened him. To this purpose he said that the gods watch over men more attentively than the vulgar imagine; for they believe there are some things which the gods observe and others which they pass by unregarded; but he held that the gods observe all our actions and all our words, that they penetrate even into our most secret thoughts, that they are present at all our deliberations, and that they inspire us in all our affairs.

It is astonishing, therefore, to consider how the Athenians could suffer themselves to be persuaded that Socrates entertained any unworthy thoughts of the Deity; he who never let slip one single word against the respect due to the gods, nor was ever guilty of any action that savoured in the least of impiety; but who, on the contrary, has done and said things that could not proceed but from a mind truly pious, and that are sufficient to gain a man an eternal reputation of piety and virtue.

CHAPTER II

SOCRATES NOT A DEBAUCHER OF YOUTH

WHAT surprises me yet more is, that some could believe that Socrates was a debaucher of young men! Socrates the most sober and most chaste of all men, who cheerfully supported both cold and heat; whom no inconvenience, no hardships, no labours could startle, and who had learned to wish for so little, that though he had scarce anything, he had always enough. Then how could he teach impiety, injustice, gluttony, impurity, and luxury? And so far was he from doing so, that he reclaimed many persons from those vices, inspiring them with the love of virtue, and putting them in hopes of coming to preferment in the world, provided they would take a little care of themselves. Yet he never promised any man to teach him to be virtuous; but as he made a public profession of virtue, he created in the minds of those who frequented him the hopes of becoming virtuous by his example.

He neglected not his own body, and praised not those that neglected theirs. In like manner, he blamed the custom of some who eat too much, and afterwards use violent exercises; but he approved of eating till nature be satisfied, and of a moderate exercise after it, believing that method to be an advantage to health, and proper to unbend and divert the mind. In his clothes he was neither nice nor costly; and what I say of his clothes ought likewise to be understood of his whole way of living. Never any of his friends became covetous in his conversation, and he reclaimed them from that sordid disposition, as well as from all others; for he would accept of no gratuity from any who desired to confer with him, and said that was the way to discover a noble and generous heart, and that they who take rewards betray a meanness of soul, and sell their own persons, because they impose on themselves a necessity of instructing those from whom they receive a salary. He wondered, likewise, why a man, who promises to teach virtue, should ask money; as if he believed not the greatest of all gain to consist in the acquisition of a good friend, or, as if he feared, that he who, by his means, should become virtuous, and be obliged to him for so great a benefit, would not be sufficiently grateful for it. Quite different from Socrates, who never boasted of any such thing, and who was most certain that all who heard him and received his maxims would love him for ever, and be capable of loving others also. After this, whosoever says that such a man debauched the youth, must at the same time say that the study of virtue is debauchery.

But the accuser says that Socrates taught to despise the constitution that was established in the Republic, because he affirmed it to be a folly to elect magistrates by lots; since if anyone had occasion for a pilot, a musician, or an architect, he would not trust to chance for any such person, though the faults that can be committed by men in such capacities are far from being of so great importance as those that are committed in the government of the Republic. He says, therefore, that such arguments insensibly accustom the youth to despise the laws, and render them more audacious and more violent. But, in my opinion, such as study the art of prudence, and who believe they shall be able to render themselves capable of giving good advice and counsel to their fellow-citizens, seldom become men of violent tempers; because they know that violence is hateful and full of danger; while, on the contrary, to win by persuasion is full of love and safety. For they, whom we have compelled, brood a secret hatred against us, believing we have done them wrong; but those whom we have taken the trouble to persuade continue our friends, believing we have done them a kindness. It is not, therefore, they who apply themselves to the study of prudence that become violent, but those brutish untractable tempers who have much power in their hands and but little judgment to manage it. ———— He farther said that when a man desires to carry anything by force, he must have many friends to assist him: as, on the contrary, he that can persuade has need of none but himself, and is not subject to shed blood; for who would rather choose to kill a man than to make use of his services, after having gained his friendship and good-will by mildness?

The accuser adds, in proof of the ill tendency of the doctrine of Socrates, that Critias and Alcibiades, who were two of his most intimate friends, were very bad men, and did much mischief to their country. For Critias was the most insatiable and cruel of all the thirty tyrants; and Alcibiades the most dissolute, the most insolent, and the most audacious citizen that ever the Republic had. As for me, I pretend not to justify them, and will only relate for what reason they frequented Socrates. They were men of an unbounded ambition, and who resolved, whatever it cost, to govern the State, and make themselves be talked of. They had heard that Socrates lived very content upon little or nothing, that he entirely commanded his passions, and that his reasonings were so persuasive that he drew all men to which side he pleased. Reflecting on this, and being of the temper we mentioned, can it be thought that they desired the acquaintance of Socrates, because they were in love with his way of life, and with his temperance, or because they believed that by conversing with him they should render themselves capable of reasoning aright, and of well-managing the public affairs? For my part, I believe that if the gods had proposed to them to live always like him, or to die immediately, they would rather have chosen a sudden death. And it is easy to judge this from their actions; for as soon as they thought themselves more capable than their companions, they forsook Socrates, whom they had frequented, only for the purpose I mentioned, and threw themselves wholly into business.

It may, perhaps, be objected that he ought not to have discoursed to his friends of things relating to the government of the State, till after he had taught them to live virtuously. I have nothing to say to this; but I observe that all who profess teaching do generally two things: they work in presence of their scholars, to show them how they ought to do, and they instruct them likewise by word of mouth. Now, in either of these two ways, no man ever taught to live well, like Socrates; for, in his whole life, he was an example of untainted probity; and in his discourses he spoke of virtue and of all the duties of man in a manner that made him admired of all his hearers. And I know too very well that Critias and Alcibiades lived very virtuously as long as they frequented him; not that they were afraid of him, but because they thought it most conducive to their designs to live so at that time.

Many who pretend to philosophy will here object, that a virtuous person is always virtuous, and that when a man has once come to be good and temperate, he will never afterwards become wicked nor dissolute; because habitudes that can be acquired, when once they are so, can never more be effaced from the mind. But I am not of this opinion; for as they who use no bodily exercises are awkward and unwieldy in the actions of the body, so they who exercise not their minds are incapable of the noble actions of the mind, and have not courage enough to undertake anything worthy of praise, nor command enough over themselves to abstain from things that are forbidden. For this reason, parents, though they be well enough assured of the good natural disposition of their children, fail not to forbid them the conversation of the vicious, because it is the ruin of worthy dispositions, whereas the conversation of good men is a continual meditation of virtue. Thus a poet says,

> "By those whom we frequent, we're ever led:
> Example is a law by all obeyed,
> Thus with the good, we are to good inclined,
> But vicious company corrupts the mind."

And another in like manner:

> "Virtue and vice in the same man are found,
> And now they gain, and now they lose their ground."

And, in my opinion, they are in the right: for when I consider that they who have learned verses by heart forget them unless they repeat them often, so I believe that they who neglect the reasonings of philosophers, insensibly lose the remembrance of them; and when they have let these excellent notions slip out of their minds, they at the same time lose the idea of the things that supported in the soul the love of temperance; and, having forgot those things, what wonder is it if at length they forget temperance likewise?

I observe, besides, that men who abandon themselves to the debauches of wine or women find it more difficult to apply themselves to things that are profitable, and to abstain from what is hurtful. For many who live frugally before they fall in love become prodigal when that passion gets the mastery over them; insomuch that after having wasted their estates, they are reduced to gain their bread by methods they would have been ashamed of before. What hinders then, but that a man, who has been once temperate, should be so no longer, and that he who has led a good life at one time should not do so at another? I should think, therefore, that the being of all virtues, and chiefly of temperance, depends on the practice of them: for lust, that dwells in the same body with the soul, incites it continually to despise this virtue, and to find out the shortest way to gratify the senses only.

Thus, whilst Alcibiades and Critias conversed with Socrates, they were able, with so great an assistance, to tame their inclinations; but after they had left him, Critias, being retired into Thessaly, ruined himself entirely in the company of some libertines; and Alcibiades, seeing himself courted by several women of quality, because of his beauty, and suffering himself to be corrupted by soothing flatterers, who made their court to him, in consideration of the credit he had in the city and with the allies; in a word, finding himself respected by all the Athenians, and that no man disputed the first rant with him, began to neglect himself, and acted like a great wrestler, who takes not the trouble to exercise himself, when he no longer finds an adversary who dares to contend with him.

If we would examine, therefore, all that has happened to them; if we consider how much the greatness of their birth, their interest, and their riches, had puffed up their minds; if we reflect on the ill company they fell into, and the many opportunities they had of debauching themselves, can we be surprised that, after they had been so long absent from Socrates, they arrived at length to that height of insolence to which they have been seen to arise? If they have been guilty of crimes, the accuser will load Socrates with them, and not allow him to be worthy of praise, for having kept them within the bounds of their duty during their youth, when, in all appearance, they would have been the most disorderly and least governable. This, however, is not the way we judge of other things; for whoever pretended that a musician, a player on the lute, or any other person that teaches, after he has made a good scholar, ought to be blamed for his growing more ignorant under the care of another master? If a young man gets an acquaintance that brings him into debauchery, ought his father to lay the blame on the first friends of his son among whom he always lived virtuously? Is it not true, on the contrary, that the more he finds that this last friendship proves destructive to him, the more reason he will have to praise his former acquaintance. And are the fathers themselves, who are daily with their children, guilty of their faults, if they give them no ill example? Thus they ought to have judged of Socrates; if he led an ill life, it was reasonable to esteem him vicious; but if a good, was it just to accuse him of crimes of which he was innocent?

And yet he might have given his adversaries ground to accuse him, had he but approved, or seemed to approve those vices in others, from which he kept himself free: but Socrates abhorred vice, not only in himself, but in everyone besides. To prove which, I need only relate his conduct toward Critias, a man extremely addicted to debauchery. Socrates perceiving that this man had an unnatural passion for Euthydemus, and that the violence of it would precipitate him so far a length as to make him transgress the bounds of nature, shocked at his behaviour, he exerted his utmost strength of reason and argument to dissuade him from so wild a desire. And while the impetuosity of Critias' passion seemed to scorn all check or control, and the modest rebuke of Socrates had been disregarded, the philosopher, out of an ardent zeal for virtue, broke out in such language, as at once declared his own strong inward sense of decency and order, and the monstrous shame-fulness of Critias' passion. Which severe but just reprimand of Socrates, it is thought, was the foundation of that grudge which he ever after bore him; for during the tyranny of the Thirty, of which Critias was one, when, together with Charicles, he had the care of the civil government of the city, he failed not to remember this affront, and, in revenge of it, made a law to forbid teaching the art of reasoning in Athens: and having nothing to reproach Socrates with in particular, he laboured to render him odious by aspersing him with the usual calumnies that are thrown on all philosophers: for I have never heard Socrates say that he taught this art, nor seen any man who ever heard him say so; but Critias had taken offence, and gave sufficient proofs of it: for after the Thirty had caused to be put to death a great number of the citizens, and even of the most eminent, and had let loose the reins to all sorts of violence and rapine, Socrates said in a certain place that he wondered very much that a man who keeps a herd of cattle, and by his ill conduct loses every day some of them, and suffers the others to fall away, would not own himself to be a very ill keeper of his herd; and that he should wonder yet more if a Minister of State, who lessens every day the number of his citizens, and makes the others more dissolute, was not ashamed of his ministry, and would not own himself to be an ill magistrate. This was reported to Critias and Charicles, who forthwith sent for Socrates, and showing him the law they had made, forbid him to discourse with the young men. Upon which Socrates asked them whether they would permit him to propose a question, that he might be informed of what he did not understand in this prohibition; and his request being granted, he spoke in this manner:

"I am most ready to obey your laws; but that I may not transgress through ignorance, I desire to know of you, whether you condemn the art of reasoning, because you believe it consists in saying things well, or in saying them ill? If for the former reason, we must then, from henceforward, abstain from speaking as we ought; and if for the latter, it is plain that we ought to endeavour to speak well."

At these words Charicles flew into a passion, and said to him: "Since you pretend to be ignorant of things that are so easily known, we forbid you to speak to the young men in any manner whatever."

"It is enough," answered Socrates; "but that I may not be in a perpetual uncertainty, pray prescribe to me, till what age men are young."

"Till they are capable of being members of the Senate," said Charicles: "in a word, speak to no man under thirty years of age."

"How!" says Socrates, "if I would buy anything of a tradesman who is not thirty years old am I forbid to ask him the price of it?"

"I mean not so," answered Charicles: "but I am not surprised that you ask me this question, for it is your custom to ask many things that you know very well."

Socrates added: "And if a young man ask me in the street where Charicles lodges, or whether I know where Critias is, must I make him no answer?"

"I mean not so neither," answered Charicles.

Here Critias, interrupting their discourse, said: "For the future, Socrates, you must have nothing to do with the city tradesmen, the shoemakers, masons, smiths, and other mechanics, whom you so often allege as examples of life; and who, I apprehend, are quite jaded with your discourses."

"I must then likewise," replied Socrates, "omit the consequences I draw from those discourses; and have no more to do with justice, piety, and the other duties of a good man."

"Yes, yes," said Charicles; "and I advise you to meddle no more with those that tend herds of oxen; otherwise take care you lose not your own." And these last words made it appear that Critias and

Charicles had taken offence at the discourse which Socrates had held against their government, when he compared them to a man that suffers his herd to fall to ruin.

Thus we see how Critias frequented Socrates, and what opinion they had of each other. I add, moreover, that we cannot learn anything of a man whom we do not like: therefore if Critias and Alcibiades made no great improvement with Socrates, it proceeded from this, that they never liked him. For at the very time that they conversed with him, they always rather courted the conversation of those who were employed in the public affairs, because they had no design but to govern.—The following conference of Alcibiades, in particular, which he had with Pericles, his governor—who was the chief man of the city, whilst he was yet under twenty years of age—concerning the nature of the laws, will confirm what I have now advanced.

"Pray," says Alcibiades, "explain to me what the law is: for, as I hear men praised who observe the laws, I imagine that this praise could not be given to those who know not what the law is."

"It is easy to satisfy you," answered Pericles: the law is only what the people in a general assembly ordain, declaring what ought to be done, and what ought not to be done."

"And tell me," added Alcibiades, "do they ordain to do what is good, or what is ill?"

"Most certainly what is good." Alcibiades pursued: "And how would you call what a small number of citizens should ordain, in states where the people is not the master, but all is ordered by the advice of a few persons, who possess the sovereignty?" "I would call whatever they ordain a law; for laws are nothing else but the ordinances of sovereigns." "If a tyrant then ordain anything, will that be a law?"

"Yes, it will," said Pericles.

"But what then is violence and injustice?" continued Alcibiades; "is it not when the strongest makes himself be obeyed by the weakest, not by consent, but by force only?" "In my opinion it is."

"It follows then," says Alcibiades, "that ordinances made by a prince, without the consent of the citizens, will be absolutely unjust."

"I believe so," said Pericles; "and cannot allow that the ordinances of a prince, when they are made without the consent of the people, should bear the name of laws." "And what the chief citizens ordain, without procuring the consent of the greater number, is that likewise a violence?"

"There is no question of it," answered Pericles; "and in general, every ordinance made without the consent of those who are to obey it, is a violence rather than a law." "And is what the populace decree, without the concurrence of the chiefs, to be counted a violence likewise, and not a law?"

"No doubt it is," said Pericles: "but when I was of your age, I could resolve all these difficulties, because I made it my business to inquire into them, as you do now."

"Would to God," cried Alcibiades, "I had been so happy as to have conversed with you then, when you understood these matters better." To this purpose was their dialogue.

Critias and Alcibiades, however, continued not long with Socrates, after they believed they had improved themselves, and gained some advantages over the other citizens: for besides that they thought not his conversation very agreeable, they were displeased that he took upon him to reprimand them for their faults; and thus they threw themselves immediately into the public affairs, having never had any other design but that. The usual companions of Socrates were Crito, Chaerephon, Chaerecrates, Simmias, Cebes, Phaedon, and some others; none of whom frequented him that they might learn to speak eloquently, either in the assemblies of the people, or in the courts of justice before the judges; but that they might become better men, and know how to behave themselves towards their domestics, their relations, their friends, and their fellow-citizens. All these persons led very innocent lives; and, whether we consider them in their youth or examine their behaviour in a more advanced age, we shall find that they never were guilty of any bad action, nay, that they never gave the least ground to suspect them of being so.

But the accuser says that Socrates encouraged children to despise their parents, making them believe that he was more capable to instruct them than they; and telling them that as the laws permit a man to chain his own father if he can convict him of lunacy, so, in like manner, it is but just that a man of excellent sense should throw another into chains who has not so much understanding. I cannot deny but that Socrates may have said something like this; but he meant it not in the sense in which the accuser would have it taken: and he fully discovered what his meaning by these words was, when he said that he who should pretend to chain others because of their ignorance, ought, for the same reason, to submit to be chained himself by men who know more than he. Hence it is that he argued so often of the difference between folly and ignorance; and then he plainly said that fools and madmen ought to be chained indeed, as well for their own interest as for that of their friends; but that they who are ignorant of things they should know, ought only to be instructed by those that understand them.

The accuser goes on, that Socrates did not only teach men to despise their parents, but their other relations too; because he said that if a man be sick, or have a suit in law, it is not his relations, but the physicians, or the advocates who are of use to him. He further alleged that Socrates, speaking of friends, said it was to no purpose to bear good-will to any man, if it be not in our power to serve him; and that the only friends whom we ought to value are they who know what is good for us, and can teach it to us: thus, says the accuser, Socrates, by persuading the youth that he was the wisest of all men, and the most capable to set others in the right road to wisdom, made them believe that all the rest of mankind were nothing in comparison with him. I remember, indeed, to have heard him sometimes talk after this manner of parents, relations, and friends; and he observed besides, if I mistake not, that when the soul, in which the understanding resides, is gone out of the body, we soon bury the corpse; and even though it be that of our nearest relation, we endeavour to put it out of our sight as

19

soon as decently we can. Further, though every man loves his own body to a great degree, we scruple not nevertheless to take from it all that is superfluous: for this reason we cut our hair and our nails, we take off our corns and our warts, and we put ourselves into the surgeons' hands, and endure caustics and incisions; and after they have made us suffer a great deal of pain, we think ourselves obliged to give them a reward: thus, too, we spit, because the spittle is of no use in the mouth, but on the contrary is troublesome. But Socrates meant not by these, or the like sayings, to conclude that a man ought to bury his father alive, or that we ought to cut off our legs and arms; but he meant only to teach us that what is useless is contemptible, and to exhort every man to improve and render himself useful to others; to the end that if we desire to be esteemed by our father, our brother, or any other relation, we should not rely so much on our parentage and consanguinity, as not to endeavour to render ourselves always useful to those whose esteem we desire to obtain.

The accuser says further against Socrates, that he was so malicious as to choose out of the famous poets the passages that contained the worst instructions, and that he made use of them in a sly manner, to inculcate the vices of injustice and violence: as this verse of Hesiod,

"Blame no employment, but blame idleness."

And he pretends that Socrates alleged this passage to prove that the poet meant to say that we ought not to count any employment unjust or dishonourable, if we can make any advantage of it. This, however, was far from the thoughts of Socrates; but, as he had always taught that employment and business are useful and honourable to men, and that idleness is an evil, he concluded that they who busy themselves about anything that is good are indeed employed; but that gamesters and debauched persons, and all who have no occupations, but such as are hurtful and wicked, are idle. Now, in this sense, is it not true to say:—

"Blame no employment, but blame idleness"?

The accuser likewise says that Socrates often repeated, out of Homer, a speech of Ulysses; and from thence he concludes that Socrates taught that the poet advised to beat the poor and abuse the common people. But it is plain Socrates could never have drawn such a wild and unnatural inference from those verses of the poet, because he would have argued against himself, since he was as poor as anyone besides. What he meant, therefore, was only this, that such as are neither men of counsel nor execution, who are neither fit to advise in the city nor to serve in the army, and are nevertheless proud and insolent, ought to be brought to reason, even though they be possessed of great riches. And this was the true meaning of Socrates, for he loved the men of low condition, and expressed a great civility for all sorts of persons; insomuch that whenever he was consulted, either by the Athenians or by foreigners, he would never take anything of any man for the instructions he gave them, but imparted his wisdom freely, and without reward, to all the world; while they, who became rich by his liberality, did not afterwards behave themselves so generously, but sold very dear to others what had cost them nothing; and, not being of so obliging a temper as he, would not impart their knowledge to any who had it not in their power to reward them. In short, Socrates has rendered the city of Athens famous throughout the whole earth; and, as Lychas was said to be the honour of Sparta, because he treated, at his own expense, all the foreigners who came to the feasts of the Gymnopaedies, so it may, with much greater reason, be said of Socrates that he was the glory of Athens, he who all his life made a continual distribution of his goodness and virtues, and who, keeping open for all the world the treasures of an inestimable wealth, never sent any man out of his company but more virtuous, and more improved in the principles of honour, than formerly he was. Therefore, in my opinion, if he had been treated according to his merit, they should have decreed him public honours rather than have condemned him to an infamous death. For against whom have the laws ordained the punishment of death? Is it not for thieves, for robbers, for men guilty of sacrilege, for those who sell persons that are free? But where, in all the world, can we find a man more innocent of all those crimes than Socrates? Can it be said of him that he ever held correspondence with the enemy, that he ever fomented any sedition, that he ever was the cause of a rebellion, or any other the like mischiefs? Can any man lay to his charge that he ever detained his estate, or did him or it the least injury? Was he ever so much as suspected of any of these things? How then is it possible he should be guilty of the crimes of which he was accused; since, instead of not believing in the gods, as the accuser says, it is manifest he was a sincere adorer of them? Instead of corrupting the youth, as he further alleges against him, he made it his chief care to deliver his friends from the power of every guilty passion, and to inspire them with an ardent love for virtue, the glory, the ornament, and felicity of families as well as of states? And this being fact (and fact it is, for who can deny it?), is it not certain that the Republic was extremely obliged to him, and that she ought to have paid him the highest honours?

CHAPTER III

HOW SOCRATES BEHAVED THROUGH THE WHOLE OF HIS LIFE

HAVING, therefore, observed myself that all who frequented him improved themselves very much in his conversation, because he instructed them no less by his example than by his discourses, I am resolved to set down, in this work, all that I can recollect both of his actions and words.

First, then, as to what relates to the service of the gods, he strictly conformed to the advice of the oracle, who never gives any other answer to those who inquire of him in what manner they ought to sacrifice to the gods, or what honours they ought to render to the dead, than that everyone should observe the customs of his own country. Thus in all the acts of religious worship Socrates took particular care to do nothing contrary to the custom of the Republic, and advised his friends to make that the rule of their devotion to the gods, alleging it to be an argument of superstition and vanity to dissent from the established worship.

When he prayed to the gods he besought them only to give him what is good, because they know better than we do what things are truly good for us; and he said that men who pray for silver, or for gold, or for the sovereign authority, made as foolish requests as if they prayed that they might play or fight, or desired any other thing whose event is uncertain, and that might be likely to turn to their disadvantage.

When he offered sacrifices he did not believe that his poverty rendered them despicable in the presence of the gods; and, while he offered according to his ability, he thought he gave as much as the rich, who load the altars with costly gifts, for he held that it would be an injustice in the gods to take more delight in costly sacrifices than in poorer ones, because it would then follow that the offerings of the wicked would for the most part be more acceptable to them than the gifts of the good; and that, if this were so, we ought not to desire to live one moment longer: he thought, therefore, that nothing was so acceptable to the Deity as the homage that is paid him by souls truly pious and innocent. To this purpose he often repeated these verses: —

> "Offer to heaven according to thy pow'r:
> Th' indulgent gracious gods require no more."

And not only in this, but in all the other occasions of life, he thought the best advice he could give his friends was to do all things according to their ability.

When he believed that the gods had admonished him to do anything, it was as impossible to make him take a contrary resolution as it would have been to have prevailed with him in a journey to change a guide that was clear-sighted for one that knew not the way, and was blind likewise. For this reason he pitied their folly, who, to avoid the derision of men, live not according to the admonitions and commands of the gods; and he beheld with contempt all the subtilties of human prudence when he compared them with divine inspirations.

His way of living was such that whoever follows it may be assured, with the help of the gods, that he shall acquire a robust constitution and a health not to be easily impaired; and this, too, without any great expense, for he was content with so little that I believe there was not in all the world a man who could work at all but might have earned enough to have maintained him. He generally ate as long as he found pleasure in eating, and when he sat down to table he desired no other sauce but a sound appetite. All sorts of drink were alike pleasing to him, because he never drank but when he was thirsty; and if sometimes he was invited to a feast, he easily avoided eating and drinking to excess, which many find very difficult to do in those occasions. But he advised those who had no government of themselves never to taste of things that tempt a man to eat when he is no longer hungry, and that excite him to drink when his thirst is already quenched, because it is this that spoils the stomach, causes the headache, and puts the soul into disorder. And he said, between jest and earnest, that he believed it was with such meats as those that Circe changed men into swine, and that Ulysses avoided that transformation by the counsel of Mercury, and because he had temperance enough to abstain from tasting them.

As to love, his advice, was to avoid carefully the company of beautiful persons, saying it was very difficult to be near them and escape being taken in the snare; and, having been told that Critobulus had given a kiss to the son of Alcibiades, who was a very handsome youth, he held this discourse to Xenophon, in the presence of Critobulus himself.

"Tell me, Xenophon, what opinion have you hitherto had of Critobulus? Have you placed him in the rank of the temperate and judicious; or with the debauched and imprudent?"

"I have always looked upon him," answered Xenophon, "to be a very virtuous and prudent man."

"Change your opinion," replied Socrates, "and believe him more rash than if he threw himself on the points of naked swords or leapt into the fire."

"And what have you seen him do," said Xenophon, "that gives you reason to speak thus of him?

"Why, he had the rashness," answered Socrates, "to kiss the son of Alcibiades, who is so beautiful and charming."

"And is this all?" said Xenophon; "for my part, I think I could also willingly expose myself to the same danger that he did."

"Wretch, that you are!" replied Socrates. "Do you consider what happens to you after you have kissed a beautiful face? Do you not lose your liberty? Do you not become a slave? Do you not engage yourself in a vast expense to procure a sinful pleasure? Do you not find yourself in an incapacity of doing what is good, and that you subject yourself to the necessity of employing your whole time and person in the pursuit of what you would despise, if your reason were not corrupted?"

"Good God!" cried Xenophon, "this is ascribing a wonderful power to a kiss forsooth."

"And are you surprised at it?" answered Socrates. "Are there not some small animals whose bite is so venomous that it causes insufferable pain, and even the loss of the senses?"

"I know it very well," said Xenophon, "but these animals leave a poison behind them when they sting."

"And do you think, you fool," added Socrates, "that kisses of love are not venomous, because you perceive not the poison? Know that a beautiful person is a more dangerous animal than scorpions, because these cannot wound unless they touch us; but beauty strikes at a distance: from what place soever we can but behold her, she darts her venom upon us, and overthrows our judgment. And perhaps for this reason the Loves are represented with bows and arrows, because a beautiful face wounds us from afar. I advise you, therefore, Xenophon, when you chance to see a beauty to fly from it, without looking behind you. And for you, Critobulus, I think it convenient that you should enjoin yourself a year's absence, which will not be too long a time to heal you of your wound."

As for such as have not strength enough to resist the power of love, he thought that they ought to consider and use it as an action to which the soul would never consent, were it not for the necessity of the body; and which, though it be necessary, ought, nevertheless, to give us no inquietude. As for himself, his continence was known to all men, and it was more easy for him to avoid courting the most celebrated beauties, than it is for others to get away from disagreeable objects.

Thus we see what was his way of life in eating, drinking, and in the affair of love. He believed, however, that he tasted of those pleasures no less than they who give themselves much trouble to enjoy them; but that he had not, like them, so frequent occasions for sorrow and repentance.

CHAPTER IV

SOCRATES PROVETH THE EXISTENCE OF A DEITY

IF there be any who believe what some have written by conjecture, that Socrates was indeed excellent in exciting men to virtue, but that he did not push them forward to make any great progress in it, let such reflect a little on what he said, not only when he endeavoured to refute those that boasted they knew all things, but likewise in his familiar conversations, and let them judge afterwards if he was incapable to advance his friends in the paths of virtue.

I will, in the first place, relate a conference which he had with Aristodemus, surnamed the Little, touching the Deity, for he had heard that he never sacrificed to the gods; that he never addressed himself to them in prayer; that he never consulted the oracles, and even laughed at those that practised these things, he took him to talk in this manner:—

"Tell me, Aristodemus, are there any persons whom you value on account of their merit?"

He answered, "Yes, certainly."

"Tell me their names," added Socrates.

Aristodemus replied: "For epic poetry I admire Homer as the most excellent; for dithyrambics, Melanippides; Sophocles for tragedy; Polycletes for statuary; and Zeuxis for painting."

"Which artists," said Socrates, "do you think to be most worthy of your esteem and admiration: they who make images without soul and motion, or they who make animals that move of their own accord, and are endowed with understanding?"

"No doubt the last," replied Aristodemus, "provided they make them not by chance, but with judgment and prudence."

Socrates went on: "As there are some things which we cannot say why they were made, and others which are apparently good and useful, tell me, my friend, whether of the two you rather take to be the work of prudence than of hazard."

"It is reasonable," said Aristodemus, "to believe that the things which are good and useful are the workmanship of reason and judgment."

"Do not you think then," replied Socrates, "that the first Former of mankind designed their advantage when he gave them the several senses by which objects are apprehended; eyes for things visible, and ears for sounds? Of what advantage would agreeable scents have been to us if nostrils suited to their reception had not been given? And for the pleasures of the taste, how could we ever have enjoyed these, if the tongue had not been fitted to discern and relish them? Further, does it not appear to you wisely provided that since the eye is of a delicate make, it is guarded with the eyelid drawn back when the eye is used, and covering it in sleep? How well does the hair at the extremity of the eyelid keep out dust, and the eyebrow, by its prominency, prevent the sweat of the forehead from running into the eye to its hurt. How wisely is the ear formed to receive all sorts of sounds, and not to be filled with any to the exclusion of others. Are not the fore teeth of all animals fitted to cut off proper portions of food, and their grinders to reduce it to a convenient smallness? The mouth, by which we take in the food we like, is fitly placed just beneath the nose and eyes, the judges of its goodness; and what is offensive and disagreeable to our senses is, for that reason, placed at a proper distance from them. In short, these things being disposed in such order, and with so much care, can you hesitate one moment to determine whether it be an effect of providence or of chance?"

"I doubt not of it in the least," replied Aristodemus, "and the more I fix my thoughts on the contemplation of these things the more I am persuaded that all this is the masterpiece of a great workman, who bears an extreme love to men."

"What say you," continued Socrates, "to this, that he gives all animals a desire to engender and propagate their kind; that he inspires the mothers with tenderness and affection to bring up their young; and that, from the very hour of their birth, he infuses into them this great love of life and this mighty aversion to death?"

"I say," replied Aristodemus, "that it is an effect of his great care for their preservation."

"This is not all," said Socrates, "answer me yet farther; perhaps you would rather interrogate me. You are not, I persuade myself, ignorant that you are endowed with understanding; do you then think that there is not elsewhere an intelligent being? Particularly, if you consider that your body is only a little earth taken from that great mass which you behold. The moist that composes you is only a small drop of that immense heap of water that makes the sea; in a word, your body contains only a small part of all the elements, which are elsewhere in great quantity. There is nothing then but your understanding alone, which, by a wonderful piece of good fortune, must have come to you from I know not whence, if there were none in another place; and can it then be said that all this universe and all these so vast and numerous bodies have been disposed in so much order, without the help of an intelligent Being, and by mere chance?"

"I find it very difficult to understand it otherwise," answered Aristodemus, "because I see not the gods, who, you say, make and govern all things, as I see the artificers who do any piece of work amongst us."

"Nor do you see your soul neither," answered Socrates, "which governs your body; but, because you do not see it, will you from thence infer you do nothing at all by its direction, but that everything you do is by mere chance?

Aristodemus now wavering said, "I do not despise the Deity, but I conceive such an idea of his magnificence and self-sufficiency, that I imagine him to have no need of me or my services."

"You are quite wrong," said Socrates, "for by how much the gods, who are so magnificent, vouchsafe to regard you, by so much you are bound to praise and adore them."

"It is needless for me to tell you," answered Aristodemus, "that, if I believed the gods interested themselves in human affairs, I should not neglect to worship them."

"How!" replied Socrates, "you do not believe the gods take care of men, they who have not only given to man, in common with other animals, the senses of seeing, hearing, and taste, but have also given him to walk upright; a privilege which no other animal can boast of, and which is of mighty use to him to look forward, to remote objects, to survey with facility those above him, and to defend himself from any harm? Besides, although the animals that walk have feet, which serve them for no other use than to walk, yet, herein, have the gods distinguished man, in that, besides feet, they have given him hands, the instruments of a thousand grand and useful actions, on which account he not only excels, but is happier than all animals besides. And, further, though all animals have tongues, yet none of them can speak, like man's; his tongue only can form words, by which he declares his thoughts, and communicates them to others. Not to mention smaller instances of their care, such as the concern they take of our pleasures, in confining men to no certain season for the enjoying them, as they have done other animals.

"But Providence taketh care, not only of our bodies, but of our souls: it hath pleased the great Author of all, not only to give man so many advantages for the body, but (which is the greatest gift of all, and the strongest proof of his care) he hath breathed into him an intelligent soul, and that, too, the most excellent of all, for which of the other animals has a soul that knows the being of the Deity, by whom so many great and marvellous works are done? Is there any species but man that serves and adores him? Which of the animals can, like him, protect himself from hunger and thirst, from heat and cold? Which, like him, can find remedies for diseases, can make use of his strength, and is as capable of learning, that so perfectly retains the things he has seen, he has heard, he has known? In a word, it is manifest that man is a god in comparison with the other living species, considering the advantages he naturally has over them, both of body and soul. For, if man had a body like to that of an ox the subtilty of his understanding would avail him nothing, because he would not be able to execute what he should project. On the other hand, if that animal had a body like ours, yet, being devoid of understanding, he would be no better than the rest of the brute species. Thus the gods have at once united in your person the most excellent structure of body and the greatest perfection of soul; and now can you still say, after all, that they take no care of you? What would you have them do to convince you of the contrary?"

"I would have them," answered Aristodemus, "send on purpose to let me know expressly all that I ought to do or not to do, in like manner as you say they do give you notice."

"What!" said Socrates, "when they pronounce any oracle to all the Athenians, do you think they do not address themselves to you too, when by prodigies they make known to the Greeks the things that are to happen, are they silent to you alone, and are you the only person they neglect? Do you think that the gods would have instilled this notion into men, that it is they who can make them happy or miserable, if it were not indeed in their power to do so? And do you believe that the human race would have been thus long abused without ever discovering the cheat? Do you not know that the most ancient and wisest republics and people have been also the most pious, and that man, at the age when his judgment is ripest, has then the greatest bent to the worship of the Deity?

"My dear Aristodemus, consider that your mind governs your body according to its pleasure: in like manner we ought to believe that there is a mind diffused throughout the whole universe that disposeth of all things according to its counsels. You must not imagine that your weak sight can reach to objects that are several leagues distant, and that the eye of God cannot, at one and the same time, see all things. You must not imagine that your mind can reflect on the affairs of Athens, of Egypt, and of Sicily, and that the providence of God cannot, at one and the same moment, consider all things. As, therefore, you may make trial of the gratitude of a man by doing him a kindness, and as you may discover his prudence by consulting him in difficult affairs, so, if you would be convinced how great is the power and goodness of God, apply yourself sincerely to piety and his worship; then, my dear Aristodemus, you shall soon be persuaded that the Deity sees all, hears all, is present everywhere, and, at the same time, regulates and superintends all the events of the universe."

By such discourses as these Socrates taught his friends never to commit any injustice or dishonourable action, not only in the presence of men, but even in secret, and when they are alone, since the Divinity hath always an eye over us, and none of our actions can be hid from him.

CHAPTER V

THE PRAISE OF TEMPERANCE

AND if temperance be a virtue in man, as undoubtedly it is, let us see whether any improvement can be made by what he said of it. I will here give you one of his discourses on that subject:—

"If we were engaged in a war," said he, "and were to choose a general, would we make choice of a man given to wine or women, and who could not support fatigues and hardships? Could we believe that such a commander would be capable to defend us and to conquer our enemies? Or if we were lying on our deathbed, and were to appoint a guardian and tutor for our children, to take care to instruct our sons in the principles of virtue, to breed up our daughters in the paths of honour and to be faithful in the management of their fortunes, should we think a debauched person fit for that employment? Would we trust our flocks and our granaries in the hands of a drunkard? Would we rely upon him for the conduct of any enterprise; and, in short, if a present were made us of such a slave, should we not make it a difficulty to accept him? If, then, we have so great an aversion for debauchery in the person of the meanest servant, ought we not ourselves to be very careful not to fall into the same fault? Besides, a covetous man has the satisfaction of enriching himself, and, though he take away another's estate, he increases his own; but a debauched man is both troublesome to others and injurious to himself. We may say of him that he is hurtful to all the world, and yet more hurtful to himself, if to ruin, not only his family, but his body and soul likewise, is to be hurtful. Who, then, can take delight in the company of him who has no other diversion than eating and drinking, and who is better pleased with the conversation of a prostitute than of his friends? Ought we not, then, to practise temperance above all things, seeing it is the foundation of all other virtues; for without it what can we learn that is good, what do that is worthy of praise? Is not the state of man who is plunged in voluptuousness a wretched condition both for the body and soul; Certainly, in my opinion, a free person ought to wish to have no such servants, and servants addicted to such brutal irregularities ought earnestly to entreat Heaven that they may fall into the hands of very indulgent masters, because their ruin will be otherwise almost unavoidable."

This is what Socrates was wont to say upon this subject. But if he appeared to be a lover of temperance in his discourses, he was yet a more exact observer of it in his actions, showing himself to be not only invincible to the pleasures of the senses, but even depriving himself of the satisfaction of getting an estate; for he held that a man who accepts of money from others makes himself a servant to all their humours, and becomes their slave in a manner no less scandalous than other slaveries.

CHAPTER VI

THE DISPUTE OF SOCRATES WITH ANTIPHON, THE SOPHIST

To this end it will not be amiss to relate, for the honour of Socrates, what passed between him and the sophist Antiphon, who designed to seduce away his hearers, and to that end came to him when they were with him, and, in their presence, addressed himself to him in these words:—"I imagined, Socrates, that philosophers were happier than other men; but, in my opinion, your wisdom renders you more miserable, for you live at such a rate that no footman would live with a master that treated him in the same manner. You eat and drink poorly, you are clothed very meanly—the same suit serves you in summer and winter—you go barefoot, and for all this you take no money, though it is a pleasure to get it; for, after a man has acquired it, he lives more genteely and more at his ease. If, therefore, as in all other sorts of arts, apprentices endeavour to imitate their masters, should these who frequent your conversation become like you, it is certain that you will have taught them nothing but to make themselves miserable."

Socrates answered him in the following manner:—"You think, Antiphon, I live so poorly that I believe you would rather die than live like me. But what is it you find so strange and difficult in my way of living? You blame me for not taking money; is it because they who take money are obliged to do what they promise, and that I, who take none, entertain myself only with whom I think fit?

You despise my eating and drinking; is it because my diet is not so good nor so nourishing as yours, or because it is more scarce and dearer, or lastly, because your fare seems to you to be better? Know that a man who likes what he eats needs no other *ragoût,* and that he who finds one sort of drink pleasant wishes for no other. As to your objection of my clothes, you appear to me, Antiphon, to judge quite amiss of the matter; for, do you not know that we dress ourselves differently only because of the hot or cold weather, and if we wear shoes it is because we would walk the easier? But, tell me, did you ever observe that the cold hath hindered me from going abroad? Have you ever seen me choose the cool and fresh shades in hot weather? And, though I go barefoot, do not you see that I go wherever I will? Do you not know that there are some persons of a very tender constitution, who, by constant exercise, surmount the weakness of their nature, and at length endure fatigues better than they who are naturally more robust, but have not taken pains to exercise and harden themselves like the others? Thus, therefore, do not you believe that I, who have all my life accustomed myself to bear patiently all manner of fatigues, cannot now more easily submit to this than you, who have never thought of the matter? If I have no keen desire after dainties, if I sleep little, if I abandon not myself to any infamous amour, the reason is because. I spend my time more delightfully in things whose pleasure ends not in the moment of enjoyment, and that make me hope besides to receive an everlasting reward. Besides, you know very well, that when a man sees that his affairs go ill he is not generally very gay; and that, on the contrary, they who think to succeed in their designs, whether in agriculture, traffic, or any other undertaking, are very contented in their minds. Now, do you think that from anything whatsoever there can proceed a satisfaction equal to the inward consciousness of improving daily in virtue, and acquiring the acquaintance and friendship of the best of men? And if we were to serve our friends or our country, would not a man who lives like me be more capable of it than one that should follow that course of life which you take to be so charming?

If it were necessary to carry arms, which of the two would be the best soldier, he who must always fare deliciously, or he who is satisfied with what he finds? If they were to undergo a siege who would hold out longest, he who cannot live without delicacies, or he who requires nothing but what may easily be had? One would think, Antiphon, that you believe happiness to consist in good eating and drinking, and in an expensive and splendid way of life. For my part, I am of opinion that to have need of nothing at all is a divine perfection, and that to have need but of little is to approach very near the Deity, and hence it follows that, as there is nothing more excellent than the Deity, whatever approaches nearest to it is likewise most near the supreme excellence."

Another time Antiphon addressed himself to Socrates: "I confess you are an honest, well-meaning man, Socrates; but it is certain you know little or nothing, and one would imagine you own this to be I true, for you get nothing by your teaching. And yet, I persuade myself, you would not part with your house, or any of the furniture of it, without some gratuity, because you believe them of some small value; nay, you would not part with them for less than they are worth: if, therefore, you thought your teaching worth anything you would be paid for it according to its value; in this, indeed, you show yourself honest, because you will not, out of avarice, cheat any man, but at the same time you discover, too, that you know but little, since all your knowledge is not worth the buying."

Socrates answered him in this manner: — "There is a great resemblance between beauty and the doctrine of philosophers; what is praiseworthy in the one is so in the other, and both of them are subject to the same vice: for, if a woman sells her beauty for money, we immediately call her a prostitute; but if she knows that a man of worth and condition is fallen in love with her, and if she makes him her friend, we say she is a prudent woman. It is just the same with the doctrine of philosophers; they that sell it are sophists, and like the public women, but if a philosopher observe a youth of excellent parts, and teacheth him what he knows, in order to obtain his friendship, we say of him, that he acts the part of a good and virtuous citizen. Thus as some delight in fine horses, others in dogs, and others in birds; for my part all my delight is to be with my virtuous friends. I teach them all the good I know, and recommend them to all whom I believe capable to assist them in the way to perfection. We all draw together, out of the same fountain, the precious treasures which the ancient sages have left us; we run over their works, and if we find anything excellent we take notice of it and select it; in short, we believe we have made a great improvement when we begin to love one another." This was the answer he made, and when I heard him speak in this manner I thought him very happy, and that he effectually stirred up his hearers to the love of virtue.

Another time when Antiphon asked him why he did not concern himself with affairs of State, seeing he thought himself capable to make others good politicians? he returned this answer:— "Should I be more serviceable to the State if I took an employment whose function would be wholly bounded in my person, and take up all my time, than I am by instructing every one as I do, and in furnishing the Republic with a great number of citizens who are capable to serve her?"

CHAPTER VII

IN WHAT MANNER SOCRATES DISSUADED MEN FROM SELF-CONCEIT AND OSTENTATION

BUT let us now see whether by dissuading his friends from a vain ostentation he did not exhort them to the pursuit of virtue. He frequently said that there was no readier way to glory than to render oneself excellent, and not to affect to appear so. To prove this he alleged the following example:—"Let us suppose," said he, "that any one would be thought a good musician, without being so in reality; what course must he take? He must be careful to imitate the great masters in everything that is not of their art; he must, like them, have fine musical instruments; he must, like them, be followed by a great number of persons wherever he goes, who must be always talking in his praise. And yet he must not venture to sing in public: for then all men would immediately perceive not only his ignorance, but his presumption and folly likewise. And would it not be ridiculous in him to spend his estate to ruin his reputation? In like manner, if any one would appear a great general, or a good pilot, though he knew nothing of either, what would be the issue of it? If he cannot make others believe it, it troubles him, and if he can persuade them to think so he is yet more unhappy, because, if he be made choice of for the steering of ships, or to command an army, he will acquit himself very ill of his office, and perhaps be the cause of the loss of his best friends.

It is not less dangerous to appear to be rich, or brave, or strong, if we are not so indeed, for this opinion of us may procure us employments that are above our capacity, and if we fail to effect what was expected of us there is no remission for our faults. And if it be a great cheat to wheedle one of your neighbours out of any of his ready money or goods, and not restore them to him afterwards, it is a much greater impudence and cheat for a worthless fellow to persuade the world that he is capable to govern a Republic." By these and the like arguments he inspired a hatred of vanity and ostentation into the minds of those who frequented him.

BOOK II

CHAPTER I

A CONFERENCE OF SOCRATES
WITH ARISTIPPUS CONCERNING
PLEASURE AND TEMPERANCE

IN the same manner, likewise, he encouraged his hearers by the following arguments: to support hunger and thirst, to resist the temptations of love, to fly from laziness, and inure themselves to all manner of fatigues. For, being told that one of them lived too luxuriously, he asked him this question: "If you were entrusted, Aristippus, with the education of two young men, one to be a prince and the other a private man, how would you educate them? Let us begin with their nourishment, as being the foundation of all."

"It is true," said Aristippus, that nourishment is the foundation of our life, for a man must soon die if he be not nourished."

"You would accustom both of them," said Socrates, "to eat and drink at a certain hour?" "It is likely I should." "But which of the two," said Socrates, "would you teach to leave eating before he was satisfied, to go about some earnest business?"

"Him, without doubt," answered Aristippus, "whom I intended to render capable to govern, to the end that under him the affairs of the Republic might not suffer by delay."

"Which of the two," continued Socrates, "would you teach to abstain from drinking when he was thirsty, to sleep but little, to go late to bed, to rise early, to watch whole nights, to live chastely, to get the better of his favourite inclinations, and not to avoid fatigues, but expose himself freely to them?"

"The same still," replied Aristippus.

"And if there be any art that teaches to overcome our enemies, to which of the two is it rather reasonable to teach it?"

"To him to," said Aristippus, "for without that art all the rest would avail him nothing."

"I believe," said Socrates, "that a man, who has been educated in this manner, would not suffer himself to be so easily surprised by his enemies as the most part of animals do. For some perish by their gluttony, as those whom we allure with a bait, or catch by offering them to drink, and who fall into the snares, notwithstanding their fears and distrust. Others perish through their lasciviousness, as quails and partridges, who suffer themselves to be decoyed by the counterfeit voice of their females, and blindly following the amorous warmth that transports them, fall miserably into the nets."

"You say true," said Aristippus.

"Well, then," pursued Socrates, "is it not scandalous for a man to be taken in the same snares with irrational animals? And does not this happen to adulterers, who skulk and hide themselves in the chambers and closets of married women, though they know they run a very great risk, and that the laws are very strict and rigorous against those crimes? They know themselves to be watched, and that, if they are taken, they shall not be let go with impunity. In a word, they see punishment and infamy hanging over the heads of criminals like themselves. Besides, they are not ignorant, that there are a thousand honourable diversions to deliver them from those infamous passions, and yet they run hand over head into the midst of these dangers, and what is this but to be wretched and desperate to the highest degree?"

"I think it so," answered Aristippus.

"What say you to this," continued Socrates, "that the most necessary and most important affairs of life, as those of war and husbandry, are, with others of little less consequence, performed in the fields and in the open air, and that the greatest part of mankind accustom themselves so little to endure the inclemency of the seasons, to suffer heat and cold? Is not this a great neglect? and do you not think that a man who is to command others ought to inure himself to all these hardships?"

"I think he ought," answered Aristippus.

"Therefore," replied Socrates, "if they who are patient and laborious, as we have said, are worthy to command, may we not say that they who can do nothing of all this, ought never to pretend to any office?" Aristippus agreed to it, and Socrates went on.

"Since then you know the rank which either of these two sorts of men ought to hold, amongst which would you have us place you?"

"Me!" said Aristippus; "why truly, not amongst those that govern; for that is an office I would never choose. Let those rule who have a mind for it; for my part, I envy not their condition. For, when I reflect that we find it hard enough to supply our own wants, I do not approve of loading ourselves, besides, with the necessities of a whole people; and that being often compelled to go without many things that we desire, we should engage ourselves in an employment that would render us liable to blame, if we did not take care to supply others with everything they want: I think there is folly in all this. For republics make use of their magistrates as I do of my slaves, who shall get me my meat and drink, and all other necessaries, as I command, and not presume to touch any of it themselves; so, too, the people will have those, who govern the State, take care to provide them with plenty of all things, and will not suffer them to do anything for their own advantage. I think, therefore, that all who are pleased with a hurry of affairs, and in creating business for others, are most fit to govern, provided they have been educated and instructed in the manner we mentioned. But, for my part, I desire to lead a more quiet and easy life."

"Let us," said Socrates, "consider whether they who govern lead more happy lives than their subjects: among the nations that are known to us in Asia, the Syrians, the Phrygians, and the Lydians, are under the empire of the Persians. In Europe, the Mæotians are subject to the Scythians; in Africa, the Carthaginians reign over the rest of the Africans. Which now, in your opinion, are the most happy? Let us look into Greece, where you are at present. Whose condition, think you, is most to be desired, that of the nations who rule, or of the people who are under the dominion of others?"

"I can never," said Aristippus, "consent to be a slave; but there is a way between both that leads neither to empire nor subjection, and this is the road of liberty, in which I endeavour to walk, because it is the shortest to arrive at true quiet and repose."

"If you had said," replied Socrates, "that this way, which leads neither to empire nor subjection, is a way that leads far from all human society, you would, perhaps, have said something; for, how can we live among men, and neither command nor obey? Do you not observe that the mighty oppress the weak, and use them as their slaves, after they have made them groan under the weight of oppression, and given them just cause to complain of their cruel usage, in a thousand instances, both general and particular? And if they find any who will not submit to the yoke, they ravage their countries, spoil their corn, cut down their trees, and attack them, in short, in such a manner that they are compelled to yield themselves up to slavery, rather than undergo so unequal a war? Among private men themselves, do not the stronger and more bold trample on the weaker?"

"To the end, therefore, that this may not happen to me," said Aristippus, "I confine myself not to any republic, but am sometimes here, sometimes there, and think it best to be a stranger wherever I am."

"This invention of yours," replied Socrates, "is very extraordinary. Travellers, I believe, are not now so much infested on the roads by robbers as formerly, deterred, I suppose, by the fate of Sinnis, Scyron, Procrustes, and the rest of that gang. What then? They who are settled in their own country, and are concerned in the administration of the public affairs, they have the laws in their favours, have their relations and friends to assist them, have fortified towns and arms for their defence: over and above, they have alliances with their neighbours: and yet all these favourable circumstances cannot entirely shelter them from the attempts and surprises of wicked men. But can you, who have none of these advantages, who are, for the most part, travelling on the roads, often dangerous to most men, who never enter a town, where you have not less credit than the meanest inhabitant, and are as obscure as the wretches who prey on the properties of others; in these circumstances, can you, I say, expect to be safe, merely because you are a stranger, or perhaps have got passports from the States that promise you all manner of safety coming or going, or should it be your hard fortune to be made a slave, you would make such a bad one, that a master would be never the better for you? For, who would suffer in his family a man who would not work, and yet expected to live well? But let us see how masters use such servants.

"When they are too lascivious, they compel them to fast till they have brought them so low, that they have no great stomach to make love; if they are thieves, they prevent them from stealing, by carefully locking up whatever they could take: they chain them for fear they should run away: if they are dull and lazy, then stripes and scourges are the rewards we give them. If you yourself, my friend, had a worthless slave, would you not take the same measures with him?"

"I would treat such a fellow," answered Aristippus, "with all manner of severity, till I had brought him to serve me better. But, Socrates, let us resume our former discourse."

"In what do they who are educated in the art of government, which you seem to think a great happiness, differ from those who suffer through necessity? For you say they must accustom themselves to hunger and thirst, to endure cold and heat, to sleep little, and that they must voluntarily expose themselves to a thousand other fatigues and hardships. Now, I cannot conceive what difference there is between being whipped willingly and by force, and tormenting one's body either one way or the other, except that it is a folly in a man to be willing to suffer pain."

"How," said Socrates, "you know not this difference between things voluntary and constrained, that he who suffers hunger because he is pleased to do so may likewise eat when he has a mind; and he who suffers thirst because he is willing may also drink when he pleases. But it is not in the power of him who suffers either of them through constraint and necessity to relieve himself by eating and drinking the moment he desires it? Besides, he that voluntarily embraceth any laborious exercise finds much comfort and content in the hope that animates him. Thus the fatigues of hunting discourage not the hunters, because they hope to take the game they pursue. And yet what they take, though they think it a reward for all their toil, is certainly of very little value. Ought not they, then, who labour to gain the friendship of good men, or to overcome their enemies, or to render themselves capable of governing their families, and of serving their country, ought not these, I say, joyfully to undertake the trouble, and to rest content, conscious of the inward approbation of their own minds, and the regard and esteem of the virtuous? And to convince you that it is good to impose labours on ourselves, it is a maxim among those who instruct youth that the exercises which are easily performed at the first attempt, and which we immediately take delight in, are not capable to form the body to that vigour snd strength that is requisite in great undertakings; nor of imprinting in the soul any considerable knowledge: but that those which require patience, application, labour, and assiduity, prepare the way to illustrious actions and great achievements. This is the opinion of good judges, and of Hesiod in particular, who says somewhere —

> 'To Vice, in crowded ranks, the course we steer,
>   The road is smooth, and her abode is near;
>   But Virtue's heights are reached with sweat and pain,
>   For thus did the immortal powers ordain.
>   A long and rough ascent leads to her gate,
>   Nor, till the summit's gained, doth toil abate.'

And to the same purpose Epicharmus: —

> 'The gods confer their blessings at the price
>   Of labour——.'

Who remarks in another place —

> 'Thou son of sloth, avoid the charms of ease,
> Lest pain succeed——.'

"Of the same opinion is Prodicus, in the book he has written of the life of Hercules, where Virtue and Pleasure make their court to that hero under the appearance of two beautiful women. His words, as near as I can remember, are as follows: —

"'When Hercules,' says the moralist, 'had arrived at that part of his youth in which young men commonly choose for themselves, and show, by the result of their choice, whether they will, through the succeeding stages of their lives, enter into and walk in the path of virtue or that of vice, he went out into a solitary place fit for contemplation, there to consider with himself which of those two paths he should pursue.

"'As he was sitting there in suspense he saw two women of a larger stature than ordinary approaching towards him. One of them had a genteel and amiable aspect; her beauty was natural and easy, her person and shape clean and handsome, her eyes cast towards the ground with an agreeable reserve, her motion and behaviour full of modesty, and her raiment white as snow. The other wanted all the native beauty and proportion of the former; her person was swelled, by luxury and ease, to a size quite disproportioned and uncomely. She had painted her complexion, that it might seem fairer and more ruddy than it really was, and endeavoured to appear more graceful than ordinary in her mien, by a mixture of affectation in all her gestures. Her eyes were full of confidence, and her dress transparent, that the conceited beauty of her person might appear through it to advantage. She cast her eyes frequently upon herself, then turned them on those that were present, to see whether any one regarded her, and now and then looked on the figure she made in her own shadow.

"'As they drew nearer, the former continued the same composed pace, while the latter, striving to get before her, ran up to Hercules, and addressed herself to him in the following manner: —

"I perceive, my dear Hercules, you are in doubt which path in life you should pursue. If, then, you will be my friend and follow me, I will lead you to a path the most easy and most delightful, wherein you shall taste all the sweets of life, and live exempt from every trouble. You shall neither be concerned in war nor in the affairs of the world, but shall only consider how to gratify all your senses—your taste with the finest dainties and most delicious drink, your sight with the most agreeable objects, your scent with the richest perfumes and fragrancy of odours, how you may enjoy the embraces of the fair, repose on the softest beds, render your slumbers sweet and easy, and by what means enjoy, without even the smallest care, all those glorious and mighty blessings.

"And, for fear you suspect that the sources whence you are to derive those invaluable blessings might at some time or other fail, and that you might, of course, be obliged to acquire them at the expense of your mind and the united labour and fatigue of your body, I beforehand assure you that you shall freely enjoy all from the industry of others, undergo neither hardship nor drudgery, but have everything at your command that can afford you any pleasure or advantage."

"'Hercules, hearing the lady make him such offers, desired to know her name, to which she answered, "My friends, and those who are well acquainted with me, and whom I have conducted, call me Happiness; but my enemies, and those who would injure my reputation, have given me the name of Pleasure."

"'In the meantime, the other lady approached, and in her turn accosted him in this manner:—"I also am come to you, Hercules, to offer my assistance; I, who am well acquainted with your divine extraction and have observed the excellence of your nature, even from your childhood, from which I have reason to hope that, if you would follow the path that leadeth to my residence, you will undertake the greatest enterprises and achieve the most glorious actions, and that I shall thereby become more honourable and illustrious among mortals. But before I invite you into my society and friendship I will be open and sincere with you, and must lay down this as an established truth, that there is nothing truly valuable which can be purchased without pains and labour. The gods have set a price upon every real and noble pleasure. If you would gain the favour of the Deity you must be at the pains of worshipping Him; if you would be beloved by your friends you must study to oblige them; if you would be honoured by any city you must be of service to it; and if you would be admired by all Greece, on account of your probity and valour, you must exert yourself to do her some eminent service. If you would render your fields fruitful, and fill your arms with corn, you must labour to cultivate the soil accordingly. Would you grow rich by your herds, a proper care must be taken of them; would you extend your dominions by arms, and be rendered capable of setting at liberty your captive friends, and bringing your enemies to subjection, you must not only learn of those that are experienced in the art of war, but exercise yourself also in the use of military affairs; and if you would excel in the strength of your body you must keep your body in due subjection to your mind, and exercise it with labour and pains."

"'Here Pleasure broke in upon her discourse — "Do you see, my dear Hercules, through what long and difficult ways this woman would lead you to her promised delights? Follow me, and I will show you a much shorter and more easy way to happiness."

"Alas!" replied the Goddess of Virtue, whose visage glowed with a passion made up of scorn and pity, "what happiness can you bestow, or what pleasure can you taste, who would never do anything to acquire it? You who will take your fill of all pleasures before you feel an appetite for any; you eat before you are hungry, you drink before you are athirst; and, that you may please your taste, must have the finest artists to prepare your viands; the richest wines that you may drink with pleasure, and to give your wine the finer taste, you search every place for ice and snow luxuriously to cool it in the heat of summer. Then, to make your slumbers uninterrupted, you must have the softest down and the easiest couches, and a gentle ascent of steps to save you from any the least disturbance in mounting up to them. And all little enough, heaven knows! for you have not prepared yourself for sleep by anything you have done, but seek after it only because you have nothing to do. It is the same in the enjoyments of love, in which you rather force than follow your inclinations, and are obliged to use arts, and even to pervert nature, to keep your passions alive. Thus is it that you instruct your followers—kept awake for the greatest part of the night by debaucheries, and consuming in drowsiness all the most useful part of the day. Though immortal, you are an outcast from the gods, and despised by good men. Never have you heard that most agreeable of all sounds, your own praise, nor ever have you beheld the most pleasing of all objects, any good work of your own hands. Who would ever give any credit to anything that you say? Who would assist you in your necessity, or what man of sense would ever venture to be of your mad parties? Such as do follow you are robbed of their strength when they are young, void of wisdom when they grow old. In their youth they are bred up in indolence and all manner of delicacy, and pass their old age with difficulties and distress, full of shame for what they have done, and oppressed with the burden of what they are to do, squanderers of pleasures in their youth, and hoarders up of afflictions for their old age.

"On the contrary, my conversation is with the gods, and with good men, and there is nothing excellent performed by either without my influence. I am respected above all things by the gods and by the best of mortals, and it is just I should. I am an agreeable companion to the artisan, a faithful security to masters of families, a kind assistant to servants, a useful associate in the arts of peace, a faithful ally in the labours of war, and the best uniter of all friendships.

"My votaries, too, enjoy a pleasure in everything they either eat or drink, even without having laboured for it, because they wait for the demand of their appetites. Their sleep is sweeter than that of the indolent and inactive; and they are neither overburdened with it when they awake, nor do they, for the sake of it, omit the necessary duties of life. My young men have the pleasure of being praised by those who are in years, and those who are in years of being honoured by those who are young. They look back with comfort on their past actions, and delight themselves in their present employments. By my means they are favoured by the gods, beloved by their friends, and honoured by their country; and when the appointed period of their lives is come they are not lost in a dishonourable oblivion, but live and flourish in the praises of mankind, even to the latest posterity."

"Thus, my dear Hercules, who are descended of divine ancestors, you may acquire, by virtuous toil and industry, this most desirable state of perfect happiness."

"Such was the discourse, my friend, which the goddess had with Hercules, according to Prodicus. You may believe that he embellished the thoughts with more noble expressions than I do. I heartily wish, my dear Aristippus, that you should make such an improvement of those divine instructions, as that you too may make such a happy choice as may render you happy during the future course of your life."

CHAPTER II

SOCRATES' DISCOURSE WITH HIS ELDEST SON LAMPROCLES CONCERNING THE RESPECT DUE TO PARENTS

SOCRATES observing his eldest son Lamprocles in a rage with his mother, spoke to him in this manner:— "Come hither, my son. Have you ever heard of a certain sort of men. who are called ungrateful?"

"Very often," answered the young man.

"And do you know," said Socrates, "why they are called so?"

"We call a man ungrateful," answered Lamprocles, "who, having received a kindness, does not return the like if occasion offers."

"I think, therefore," said Socrates, "ingratitude is a kind of injustice?"

"I think so too," answered Lamprocles.

Socrates went on:— "Have you never considered of what nature this injustice is? For since it is an injustice to treat our friends ill, and on the contrary, a piece of justice to make our enemies smart for their conduct, may it be said, with like reason, that it is an injustice to be ungrateful towards our friends, and that it is just to be ungrateful towards our enemies."

"On mature consideration," answered Lamprocles, "I think it is criminal to do injustice to either of them."

"If, then," pursued Socrates, "ingratitude be an injustice, it follows that the greater the favours are which we have received, the greater is the injustice in not acknowledging them." Lamprocles granted this consequence, and Socrates continued— "Can there be any stricter obligations than those that children are laid under to their parents? For it is they who gave them a being, and who have put them in a condition to behold all the wonders of Nature, and to partake of the many good things exhibited before them by the bounty of Providence, and which are so delightful, that there is not anythng that all men more dread than to leave them; insomuch that all governments have ordained death to be the punishment of the most enormous crimes, because there is nothing can more effectually put a stop to the rage of the wicked than the apprehension of death. In the affair of marriage, it is not merely the gratification of the appetite which Nature has so strongly implanted in both sexes for their preservation that we regard; no, that passion can be satisfied in a less expensive manner, even in our streets, and other places; but when we design to enter into that state, we make choice of a woman of such a form and shape, by whom we may expect to have fine children, and of such a temper and disposition as to assure us of future happiness. When that is finished, it is then the chief care of the husband to maintain his wife, and to provide for his children things useful for life in the greatest abundance he can. On the part of the wife, many are her anxieties and troubles for the preservation of her offspring during the time of her pregnancy; she gives it then part of her nourishment and life; and after having suffered the sharpest pangs at the moment of its birth, she then gives it suck, and continues her care and love to it. All this she does to the poor helpless infant, so void of reason, that it knows not even her that is so good to it, nor can ask her for its own necessities. Full of tenderness for the welfare and happiness of her babe, her whole time, day and night, is spent in pleasing it, without the least prospect of any recompense for all her fatigue. After this, when the children are come to an age fit to be instructed, the fathers teach them all the good things they can for the conduct of their life; and if they know any man more capable to instruct them than themselves, they send them to him, without regard to the expense, thus indicating by their whole conduct what sincere pleasure it would afford them to see their children turn out men of virtue and probity."

"Undoubtedly," answered Lamprocles, "if my mother had done all this, and an hundred times as much, no man could suffer her ill-humours."

"Do not you think," said Socrates, "that the anger of a beast is much more difficult to support than that of a mother?"

"Not of a mother like her," said Lamprocles.

Socrates continued, "What strange thing has she done to you? Has she bit you, has she kicked you, as beasts do when they are angry?"

"She has a tongue that no mortal can suffer," answered Lamprocles.

"And you," replied Socrates, "how many crosses did you give her in your infancy by your continual bawling and importunate actions? how much trouble by night and by day? how much affliction in your illnesses?"

"At worst," answered Lamprocles, "I never did nor said anything that might make her blush."

"Alas!" said Socrates, "is it more difficult for you to hear in patience the hasty expressions of your mother, than it is for the comedians to hear what they say to one another on the stage when they fall into the most injurious reproaches? For they easily suffer it, knowing well that when one reviles another, he reviles him not with intent to injure him; and when one threatens another, he threatens not with design to do him any harm. You who are fully convinced likewise of the intentions of your mother, and who know very well that the hard words she gives you do not proceed from hate, but that she has a great affection for you, how can you, then, be angry with her? Is it because you imagine that she wishes you ill?"

"Not in the least," answered Lamprocles; "I never had such a thought."

"What!" continued Socrates; "a mother that loves you; a mother who, in your sickness, does all she can to recover your health, who takes care that you want for nothing, who makes so many vows to heaven for you; you say this is an ill mother? In truth, if you cannot live with her, I will say you cannot live at your ease. Tell me, in short, do you believe you ought to have any reverence or respect for any one whatever? Or do you not care for any man's favour and goodwill, neither for that of a general, suppose, or of any other magistrate?"

"On the contrary," said Lamprocles, "I am very careful to gain the goodwill of all men."

"Perhaps you would endeavour to acquire the goodwill of your neighbour, to the end he might do you kind offices, such as giving you fire when you want it, or, when any misfortune befalls you, speedily relieve you?"

"Yes, I would."

"And if you were travelling with any man, either by sea or land, would you count it a matter of indifference whether you were loved by him or not?"

"No, indeed."

"Are you then so abandoned, Lamprocles," replied Socrates, "that you would take pains to acquire the goodwill of those persons, and yet will do nothing to your mother, who loves you incomparably better than they? Know you not that the Republic concerns not herself with common instances of ingratitude; that she takes no cognisance of such crimes and that she neglects to punish those who do not return the civilities they receive? But if any one be disrespectful to his parents there is a punishment provided for such ingratitude; the laws reject him as an outlaw, and will not allow him to be received into any public office, because it is a maxim commonly received amongst us, that a sacrifice, when offered by an impious hand, cannot be acceptable to the gods, nor profitable to the Republic. Nobody can believe, that a person of such a character can be capable to perform any great or worthy action, or to act the part of a righteous judge. The same punishment is ordained likewise for those who, after the death of their parents, neglect to honour their funerals: and this is particularly examined into in the inquiry that is made into the lives of such as stand candidates for offices.

"Therefore, my son, if you be wise, you will beseech Heaven to pardon you the offences committed against your mother, to the end that the favours of the Deity may be still continued to you, and that you may not forfeit them by an ungrateful behaviour. Take care, likewise, that the public may not discover the contempt you show her, for then would you be blamed and abandoned by all the world; for, if it were suspected that you did not gratefully resent the benefits conferred on you by your parents, no man could believe you would be grateful for any kind actions that others might do you."

CHAPTER III

SOCRATES RECONCILES CHAEREPHON AND CHAERECRATES, TWO BROTHERS WHO WERE FORMERLY AT VARIANCE

Two brothers, whose names were Chaerephon and Chaerecrates, were at enmity with each other. Socrates was acquainted with them, and had a great mind to make them friends. Meeting therefore with Chaerecrates, he accosted him thus: — "Are you, too, one of those who prefer the being rich to the having a brother, and who do not consider that riches, being inanimate things, have need of being defended, whereas a brother is himself a good defence, and, after all, that there is more money than brothers? For is it not extravagant in such men to imagine that a brother does them wrong because they enjoy not his estate? Why say they not likewise, that all the world does them wrong, because they are not in possession of what belongs to the rest of mankind? But they believe, with great reason, that it is better to live in society and to be ensured of a moderate estate than to have the sole possession of all that is their neighbours', and to be exposed to the dangers that are inseparable from solitude. Nevertheless, they are not of the same opinion as to the company of their brothers. If they are rich they buy themselves slaves to serve them, they procure themselves friends to stand by them; but for their brothers they neglect them; as if a brother were not so fit to make a friend of as another person. And yet it is of great efficacy towards the begetting and establishing of friendships to have been born of the same parents and brought up together, since even beasts, we see, retain some inclination for those who have come from the same dams, and have been bred up and nourished together. Besides, a man who has a brother is the more regarded for it, and men are more cautions to offend him." Chaerecrates answered him thus:—

"You are indeed in the right to say that a good brother is a great happiness; and, unless there be a very strong cause of dissension, I think that brothers ought a little to bear with one another, and not part on a slight occasion; but when a brother fails in all things, and is quite the reverse of what he ought to be, would you have a man do what is impossible and continue in good amity with such a person?"

Socrates replied, "Does your brother give offence to all the world as well as to you? Does nobody speak well of him?"

"That," said Chaerecrates, " is one of the chief causes of the hatred I bear him, for he is sly enough to please others; but whenever we two happen to meet you would think his sole design were to fall out with me."

Socrates replied, "Does not this proceed from what I am going to say? When any man would make use of a horse, and knows not how to govern him, he can expect nothing from him but trouble. Thus, if we know not in what manner to behave ourselves toward our brother, do you think we can expect anything from him but uneasiness?"

"Why do you imagine," said Chaerecrates, "that I am ignorant in what manner I ought to carry myself to a brother, since I can show him as much love and respect, both in my words and actions, as he can show me in his? But when I see a man endeavour to disoblige me all manner of ways, shall I express any goodwill for that man? No; this is what I cannot do, and will not so much as endeavour it."

"I am astonished to hear you talk after this manner," said Socrates; "pray tell me, if you had a dog that were good to keep your flocks, who should fawn on your shepherds, and grin his teeth and snarl whenever you come in his way, whether, instead of being angry with him, you would not make much of him to bring him to know you? Now, you say that a good brother is a great happiness; you confess that you know how to oblige, and yet you put it not in practice to reconcile yourself with Chaerephon."

"I fear I have not skill enough to compass it."

"I think," said Socrates, "there will be no need of any extraordinary skill in the matter; and am certain that you have enough to engage him to wish you well, and to have a great value for you."

"Pray," cried Chaerecrates, "if you know any art I have to make myself beloved, let me know it immediately, for hitherto I never perceived any such thing."

"Answer me," said Socrates. "If you desired that one of your friends should invite you to his feast when he offered a sacrifice, what course would you take?"

"I would begin first to invite him to mine."

"And if you would engage him to take care of your affairs in your absence on a journey, what would you do?"

"I would first, during his absence, take care of his."

"And if you would have a foreigner entertain you in his family when you come into his country, what method would you take?"

"I would make him welcome at my house when he came to this town, and would endeavour to further the dispatch of his business, that he might do me the like favour when I should be in the city where he lives."

"Strange," said Socrates, "that you, who know the common methods of ingratiating yourself, will not be at the pains of practising them. Why do you scruple to begin to practise those methods? Is it because you are afraid that, should you begin with your brother, and first do him a kindness, you would appear to be of a mean-spirited and cringing disposition? Believe me, my friend, you will never, on that account, appear such. On the contrary, I take it to be the part of an heroic and generous soul to prevent our friends with kindness and our enemies with valour. Indeed, had I thought that Chaerephon had been more proper than you to propose the reconciliation, I would have endeavoured to have persuaded him to prevent you; but I take you to be more fit to manage this matter, and believe you will bring it to pass rather than he."

"What you say is absurd and unworthy of you," replied Chaerecrates. "Would you have me break the ice; I, who am the younger brother? Do you forget that among all nations the honour to begin is reserved to the elder?"

"How do you mean?" said Socrates. "Must not a younger brother give the precedency to the elder? Must he not rise up when he comes in, give him the best place, and hold his peace to let him speak? Delay, therefore, no longer to do what I desire you; go and try to appease your brother. He will receive you with open arms; it is enough that he is a friend to honour, and of a generous temper, for as there is no readier way to gain the goodwill of the mean and poor than by being liberal to them, so nothing has more influence on the mind of a man of honour and note than to treat him with respect and friendship."

Chaerecrates objected: "But when I have done what you say, if my brother should not be better tempered, what then?"

"What harm would it be to you?" said Socrates. "It will show your goodness, and that you love him, and make him appear to be ill-natured, and not deserving to be obliged by any man. But I am of opinion this will not happen, and when he sees that you attack him with civilities and good offices, I am certain he will endeavour to get the better of you in so kind and generous a contention. You are now in the most wretched condition imaginable. It is as if the hands which God has given us reciprocally to aid each other were employed only to hinder one another; or as if the feet, which by the divine providence were made to assist each other to walk, were busied only in preventing one another from going forward. Would it not, then, be a great ignorance, and at the same time a great misfortune, to turn to our disadvantage what was made only for our utility? Now, it is certain that God has given us brothers only for our good; and that two brothers are a greater advantage to one another than it can be to either of them to have two hands, two feet, two eyes, and other the like members, which are double in our body, and which Nature has designed as brothers. For the hands cannot at the same time reach two things several fathoms distant from one another; the feet cannot stretch themselves from the end of one fathom to another; the eyes, which seem to discover from so far, cannot, at the same time, see the fore and hind-part of one and the same object; but when two brothers are good friends, no distance of place can hinder them from serving each other."

CHAPTER IV

A DISCOURSE OF SOCRATES
CONCERNING FRIENDSHIP

I remember likewise a discourse which I have heard him make concerning friendship, and that may be of great use to instruct us by what means we ought to procure ourselves friends, and in what manner we should live with them. He said "that most men agree that a true friend is a precious treasure, and that nevertheless there is nothing about which we give ourselves so little trouble as to make men our friends. We take care," said he, "to buy houses, lands, slaves, flocks, and household goods, and when we have them we endeavour to keep them; but though a friend is allowed to be capable of affording us a far greater happiness than any or all of these, yet how few are solicitous to procure themselves a friend, or, when they have, to secure his friendship? Nay, some men are so stupid as to prefer their very slaves to their friends. How else can we account for their want of concern about the latter when either in distress or sickness, and at the same time their extreme anxiety for the recovery of the former when in the same condition? For then immediately physicians are sent for, and all remedies that can be thought of applied to their relief. Should both of them happen to die, they will regret more the loss of their slave than of their friend, and shed more tears over the grave of the former than of the latter. They take care of everything but their friends; they will examine into and take great notice of the smallest trifle in their affairs, which perhaps stand in no need of their care, but neglect their friends that do. In short, though they have many estates, they know them all; but though they have but few friends, yet they know not the number of them; insomuch that if they are desired to name them, they are puzzled immediately, so little are their friends in their thoughts. Nevertheless, there is nothing comparable to a good friend; no slave is so affectionate to our person or interest; no horse can render us so great service; in a word, nothing is so useful to us in all occasions. For a true friend supplies all the wants and answers all the demands of another, either in the conduct of his private affairs or in the management of the public. If, for instance, his friend be obliged to do a kindness to any man, he puts him in the way of it; if he be assaulted with any danger he immediately flies to his relief. At one time he gives him part of his estate, at another he assists him with the labour of his hands; sometimes he helps him to persuade, sometimes he aids him to compel; in prosperity he heightens his delight by rejoicing with him; in adversity he diminisheth his sorrows by bearing a share of them. The use a man may make of his hands, his eyes, his ears, his feet, is nothing at all when compared with the service one friend may render another. For often what we cannot do for our own advantage, what we have not seen, nor thought, nor heard of, when our own interests were concerned, what we have not pursued for ourselves, a friend has done for his friend. How foolish were it to be at so much trouble in cultivating a small orchard of trees, because we expect some fruit from it, and yet be at no pains to cultivate that which is instead of a whole estate—I mean Friendship—a soil the most glorious and fertile where we are sure to gather the fairest and best of fruit!"

CHAPTER V

OF THE WORTH AND VALUE OF FRIENDS

To what I have advanced above I shall here relate another discourse of his, as far as I can remember, in which he exhorted his hearers to examine themselves, that they might know what value their friends might set upon them; for seeing a man who had abandoned his friend in extreme poverty, he asked Antisthenes this question in presence of that very man and several others: "Can we set a price upon friends as we do upon slaves? One slave may be worth twenty crowns, another not worth five; such a one will cost fifty crowns, another will yield a hundred. Nay, I am told that Nicias, the son of Niceratus, gave even six hundred crowns for one slave to be inspector of his silver mines. Do you think we might likewise set prices upon friends?"

"I believe we may," answered Antisthenes; "for there are some men by whom I would rather choose to be loved than to have twenty crowns; others for whose affection I would not spend five. I know some, too, for whose friendship I would give all I am worth."

"If it be so," said Socrates, "it would be well that each man should consider how much he can be worth to his friends, and that he should endeavour to render himself as valuable as he can in their regard, to the end they might not abandon him; for when I hear one complain that his friend has betrayed him; another that he, whom he thought faithful, has preferred a small gain to the preservation of his friendship, I reflect on these stories, and ask whether, as we sell a good-for-nothing slave for what we can get for him, we are not likewise tempted to get rid of an ill-friend when we are offered more for him than he is worth? because I do not see men part with their slaves if they be good, nor abandon their friends if they be faithful."

CHAPTER VI

OF THE CHOICE OF FRIENDS

THE following conversation of Socrates with Critobulus may teach us how we ought to try friends, and with whom it is good to contract friendship:—"If we were to choose a friend," said Socrates to him, "what precaution ought we to take? Ought we not to look out for a man who is not given to luxury, to drunkenness, to women, nor to idleness? For with these vices he could never be very useful to his friend nor to himself."

"That is certain," answered Critobulus.

"Then," said Socrates, " if we found a man that loved to live great, though he had not an estate to support the expense, and who having daily occasion to employ the purses of his friends should show by his actions that whatever you lend him is so much lost, and that if you do not lend him he will take it ill of you do you not think that such a man would be very improper to make a friend of?"

"There is no doubt of it," said Critobulus.

"And if we found another," continued Socrates, "who was saving of what he had, but who, on the other hand, was so covetous that it would be quite unfit to have anything to do with him, because he would always be very ready to receive and never to give again?"

"In my opinion," said Critobulus, "this would be a worse friend than the former. And if we should find a man who was so carried away with the desire of enriching himself that he applied his mind to nothing else, but getting all he could scrape together?"

"We ought not to have anything to do with him neither," answered Critobulus, "for he would be good to no man but himself."

"If we found a quarrelsome man," continued Socrates, "who was every day like to engage all his friends in new broils and squabbles, what would you think of him?"

"That he ought to be avoided," answered Critobulus.

"And if a man," said Socrates, "were free from all these faults, and were only of a humour to desire to receive kindnesses, but never to concern himself to return them, what would you think of him?"

"That neither he, too, would be proper to make a friend of," replied Critobulus; "and indeed, after having rejected so many, I can scarce tell whom we should take."

"We ought to take," said Socrates, "a man who were the reverse of all those we have mentioned, who would be temperate in his manners, faithful in his promises, and sincere in all his actions; who would think it a point of honour not to be outdone in civilities so that it would be of advantage to have to do with him."

"But how can we be certain of all this," said Critobulus, "before we have tried him?"

"When we would give our judgment of statuaries, we have no regard," replied Socrates, "to what they say of themselves, but consider their works; and he who has already made good statues is the person of whom we have the best opinion for those he shall make for the future. Apply this to the question you asked me, and be assured that a man who has served his former friends well will be likely to show no less affection for those that come after; as we may strongly conjecture that a groom, whom we have formerly seen dress horses very well, is capable of dressing others."

"But," said Critobulus, "when we have found a man worthy of our choice, how ought we to contract a friendship with him?"

"In the first place," answered Socrates, "we must inquire whether the gods approve of it."

"But supposing they do not dissuade us, how are we to take this precious prey?"

"Not by hunting, as we catch hares," said Socrates; "nor in nets, as we take birds, nor by force, as we take our enemies; for it is very difficult to gain any man's friendship against his will, or stop him by force, and detain him in prison as a slave, seeing such ill-usage would oblige him rather to wish us ill than to love us."

"What, then, ought we to do?" pursued Critobulus.

"It is reported," replied Socrates, "that there are some words so powerful that they who know them make themselves loved by pronouncing them, and that there are likewise other charms for the same purpose."

"And where can one learn these words?" added Critobulus.

"Have you not read in Homer," answered Socrates, "what the Syrens said to enchant Ulysses? The beginning of it is thus—

'Oh, stay! oh, pride of Greece, Ulysses, stay!'

"You say true," continued Critobulus; "but did not they say as much to the others, to stop them too?"

"Not at all," said Socrates, "they enchanted with these words only the generous men who were in love with virtue."

"I begin to understand you," said Critobulus, "and seeing this charm, which is so powerful to enchant and captivate the mind, is nothing but praise, you mean that we ought to praise a man in such a manner that he may not distrust we laugh at him; otherwise, instead of gaining his affection, we shall incur his hate; for it would be insupportable to a man, who knows he is little and weak, to be praised for his graceful appearance, for being well-shaped, and of a robust constitution."

"But do you know no other charms?"

"No," answered Socrates; "but I have indeed heard it said, that Pericles knew a great many, by means of which he charmed the Republic, and gained the favour and esteem of all."

Critobulus continued, "What was it that Themistocles did to make himself so esteemed?"

"He used no other charms," said Socrates, "than the eminent services he rendered to the State."

"Which is as much as to say," replied Critobulus, "that to gain the friendship of the great, we must render ourselves capable to perform great actions."

"And could you think it possible," said Socrates, "that any one should share in the friendship of men of merit without being possessed of one good quality?"

"Why not?" answered Critobulus; "I have seen despicable rhetoricians beloved by the most famous orators, and persons who knew nothing of war live in familiarity with great generals."

"But have you seen men who are fit for nothing (for that is the question we speak of) get any friends of consequence?"

"I confess I have not," answered Critobulus; "nevertheless, since it is impossible for a man of no worth whatever to have the friendship of men of condition and merit, tell me whether the man who acquires the character of worth and merit obtains, at the same time, the friendship of all who possess that excellent character?"

"The reason, I suppose, why you ask this question," answered Socrates, "is because you frequently observe dissensions among those who equally cherish honour, and would all of them rather die than commit a base action; and you are surprised, that instead of living in friendship, they disagree among themselves, and are sometimes more difficult to reconcile than the vilest of all men."

"This is a misfortune," added Critobulus, "that arrives not among private men only; for dissensions, nay, even wars, will happen sometimes, to break out in the best-governed republics, where virtue is in the highest repute, and where vice is held in the utmost contempt. Now, when I revolve these considerations in my mind, I know not where to go in search of friends; for it is impossible, we see, for the wicked to cultivate a true friendship among themselves. Can there subsist a true and lasting friendship amongst the ungrateful, the idle, the covetous, the treacherous, and the dissolute? No, for persons of such a character will mutually expose themselves to hatred and contempt; to hatred, because of the hurtful effects of their vices; to contempt, on account of the deformity of them. Neither, on the other hand, can we expect, as you have well observed, to find friendship between a virtuous man and a person of the opposite character. For how can they who commit crimes be in good amity with those that abhor them? But what puzzles me most, my dear Socrates, is to see men of merit and virtue harassing one another, and endeavouring, to the utmost of their power, to crush and ruin their antagonists, when, in different interests, both are contending for the most lucrative posts of the Republic. I am quite at a loss to account for such a conduct on the principles of friendship; for when I daily observe the noblest affections of the mind rooted up by the sordid views of interest, I am in a great doubt whether there is any real friendship and affection, in the world."

"My dear friend," replied Socrates, "this matter is very intricate; for, if I mistake not, Nature has placed in men the principles both of friendship and dissension. Of friendship, because they have need of one another, they have compassion of their miseries, they relieve one another in their necessities, and they are grateful for the assistances which they lend one another: of dissension, because one and the same thing being agreeable to many they contend to have it, and endeavour to prejudice and thwart one another in their designs. Thus strife and anger beget war, avarice stifles benevolence, envy produces hate. But friendship overcoming all these difficulties, finds out the virtuous, and unites them together. For, out of a motive of virtue they choose rather to live quietly in a mean condition, than to gain the empire of the whole earth by the calamities of war. When they are pinched with hunger or thirst, they endure them with constancy, till they can relieve themselves without being troublesome to any one. When at any time their desires for the enjoyments of love grow violent and headstrong, then reason, or sell-government, lays hold on the reins, checks the impetuosity of the passion, keeps it within due bounds, and will not allow them to transgress the great rule of their duty. They enjoy what is lawfully their own, and are so far from usurping the rights and properties of others, that they even give them part of what they have. They agree their differences in such a manner, that all are gainers, and no man has reason to complain. They are never transported with anger so far as to commit any action of which they may afterwards repent. Envy is a passion they are ignorant of, because they live in a mutual communication of what they possess, and consider what belongs to their friends as things in their own possession. From hence you see that the virtuous do not only not oppose, but that they aid one another in the employments of the Republic; for they who seek for honours and great offices, only to have an opportunity of enriching themselves, and exercising a cruel tyranny, or to live an easy and effeminate life, are certainly very wicked and unjust, nor can they ever hope to live in friendship with any man.

"But why should he who desires not any authority, but only the better to defend himself from the wicked, or to assist his friends, or be serviceable to his country; why should such a man, I say, not agree with another, whose intentions are the same with his own? Is it because he would be less capable to serve the Republic, if he had virtuous associates in the administration of affairs? If, in the tournaments and other games, the most strong were permitted to enter into a league against the weaker, they would infallibly be victors in all the courses, and win all the prizes; for which reason they are not suffered to do so. Therefore, in affairs of State, since no man is hindered from joining with whom he pleases, to do good to the Republic, is it not more advantageous, when we concern ourselves in the government, to make friendship with men of honour and probity, who are generally, too, the most knowing and capable, and to have them for our associates than to make them our adversaries? For it is manifest, that when a man is engaged in a combat, he ought to have some to assist him, and that he will have need of a great many, if those whom he opposes be valiant and powerful. Besides, he must be liberal, and give presents to those who espouse his quarrel, to encourage them to make a more resolute and vigorous defence. Now, it is beyond all dispute, that it is much better to oblige the good, though they are but a few, than the wicked, of whom there is a great number, because the former are easily gained over to your side; whereas the latter are hardly won by the best favours, and those in the greatest abundance, too, to espouse your interest.

"However it be, Critobulus, take courage, endeavour only to become virtuous, and then boldly pursue the friendship of honest men; this is a sort of chase in which I may be helpful to you, because I am naturally inclined to love. I attack briskly those I love, and lay out all my skill to make myself beloved by them. I endeavour to kindle in their minds a flame like mine, and to make them desire my company, as ardently as I long for theirs. You stand in need of this address when you would contract a friendship with any one. Hide not, then, the secrets of your soul from me, but let me know who they are for whom you have a regard: for, having made it my study to please those who were agreeable to me, I believe that, by long experience, I have now got some considerable insight into the pursuits and ways of men."

"I have longed a great while," said Critobulus, "to learn this art, especially if it may be employed to gain me the friendship of those whose persons are not only comely and genteel, but whose minds are replenished and adorned with all virtue."

Socrates replied: "But my method forbids to use violence, and I am of opinion that all men fled from the wretch Scylla, because she detained them by force: whereas the Syrens did no violence to any man, and employed only their tuneful voices to detain those who passed near them, so that all stopped to hear, and suffered themselves to be insensibly charmed by the music of their songs."

"Be sure," said Critobulus, "that I will use no violence to them whose friendship I would gain, and therefore delay no longer to teach me your art."

"Will you give me your word likewise," said Socrates, "that you will not even give them a kiss?"

"I promise you," said Critobulus, "I will not, unless they are very beautiful persons."

"You mistake the matter," replied Socrates; "the beautiful permit not those liberties; but the ugly grant them freely enough, because they know very well that should any beauty be ascribed to them, it is only in consideration of that of the soul."

"I will not transgress in this point," said Critobulus; "only impart to me the secret you know to gain friends."

"When you would contract a friendship with any one," said Socrates, "you must give me leave to tell him that you have a great esteem for him, and that you desire to be his friend."

"With all my heart," answered Critobulus; "for sure no man can wish ill to a man who esteems him."

"And if I add besides," continued Socrates, "that because you set a great value on his merit you have much affection for his person, will you not take it amiss?"

"Not at all," said Critobulus; "for I am sensible we have a great kindness for those who bear us good-will."

"I may, then," said Socrates, "speak in that manner to those whom you desire to love: but will you likewise give me leave to advance that your greatest pleasure is to have good friends, that you take great care of them, that you behold their good actions with as much joy as if you yourself had performed them, and that you rejoice at their good fortune as much as at your own: that you are never weary when you are serving them, and that you believe it the glory of a man of honour to surpass his friends in benefits, and his enemies in valour? By this means I think I shall be very useful to you in procuring you good friends."

"Why do you ask me leave," said Critobulus, "as if you might not say of me whatever you please?"

"No, indeed," answered Socratès, "for I remember what Aspasia once said, that match-makers are successful in their business when they tell truth of the persons in whose behalf they court, but that the marriages made by their lies are unfortunate, because they who are deceived hate one another, and hate yet more the person that put them together. And therefore, for the same reason, I think I ought not to tell lies in your praise."

"You are then so far only my friend," replied Critobulus, "that if I have any good qualities to make myself be esteemed, you will assist me; if not, you will invent nothing in my behalf."

"And do you think," said Socrates, "that I should do you more service in giving you false praises, that are not your due, than by exhorting you to merit the praise of all men? If you doubt of this, consider the consequences of it. If, for instance, I should tell the owner of a ship that you are an excellent pilot, and he upon that should give you the conduct of the vessel, what hopes could you have that you should not perish? Or if I should say, publicly, that you are an experienced general, or a great politician, and if you, by that character which I should unjustly have obtained for you, should be promoted to the supreme magistracy, to what dangers would you expose your own life, and the fortune of the State? Or if I should make any private person believe that you were a good economist, and he should trust you afterwards with the care of his family, would not you be the ruin of his estate, and expose yourself to ridicule and contempt? Which is as much as to say, Critobulus, that the shortest and surest way to live with honour in the world is to be in reality what we would appear to be: and if you observe, you will find that all human virtues increase and strengthen themselves by the practice and experience of them. Take my advice, then, and labour to acquire them: but if you are of a different opinion, pray let me know it."

"I might well be ashamed," answered Critobulus, "to contradict you: for no good nor solid objection can be brought against so rational an assertion."

CHAPTER VII

SOCRATES SHOWETH ARISTARCHUS
HOW TO GET RID OF POVERTY

SOCRATES had an extreme tenderness for his friends, and if through imprudence they fell into any misfortune, he endeavoured to comfort them by his good counsels; if they laboured under poverty he did all he could to relieve them, teaching all men that they ought mutually to assist one another in necessity. I will set down some examples of his behaviour in these occasions.

Meeting Aristarchus, who looked very dejected, he said to him, "I see, Aristarchus, that something troubles you, but impart the cause of your grief to your friends, and perhaps we may comfort you."

"Indeed," said he, "I am in great affliction; for since the late troubles, many persons having fled for shelter to the Piræus, it has so fallen out that my sisters, nieces, and cousins have all thrown themselves upon me, so that I have no less than fourteen of them to maintain. You know very well that we receive no profit of our lands, the enemies being masters of the open country; our houses in the city are uninhabited, there being at present very little company in Athens; nobody will buy any goods; no man will lend money upon any interest whatever, and I believe we may as soon take it up in the middle of the streets as find where to borrow it. And I am much concerned that I shall not be able to assist my relations whom I see ready to perish, while it is impossible for me to maintain them in the present scarcity of all things."

Socrates having heard him patiently, said to him, "How comes it to pass that Ceramon, who has so many persons in his family, finds means not only to maintain them, but likewise to enrich himself by the profit he makes of them, and that you are afraid of starving to death, because you have a great many in your family?"

"The reason," answered Aristarchus, "is this, Ceramon has none but slaves to take care of, and I am to provide for persons who are free."

Socrates went on: "For which have you most esteem, for Ceramon's slaves, or for the persons who are at your house?"

"There is no comparison between them," said Aristarchus.

"Is it not then a shameful thing," replied Socrates, "that Ceramon should grow rich by means of those whom you acknowledge to be of less value, and that you should grow poor and be reduced to straits, though you keep men of condition in your house, whom you value more?"

"By no means," said Aristarchus, "there is a wide difference betwixt the two; the slaves that Ceramon keeps follow some trades, but the persons I have with me have had a liberal education and follow none."

"May not he," replied Socrates, "who knows how to do anything that is useful be said to know a trade?"

"Yes, certainly."

"And are not," continued Socrates, "oatmeal, bread, the clothes of men and women, cassocks, coats, and other the like manufactures, things very useful?"

"Without doubt."

"And do not the persons at your house know how to make any of these things?"

"On the contrary," said Aristarchus, "I believe they know how to make all of them."

"What are you then afraid of," added Socrates? "Why do you complain of poverty, since you know how to get rich? Do not you observe how wealthy Nausicides is become, what numerous herds he is master of, and what vast sums he lends the Republic? Now what made this man so rich? Why, nothing but one of those manufactures we mentioned, that of making oatmeal. You see, too, that Cirthes keeps all his family, and lives at his ease upon what he has got by being a baker. And how doth Demeas, of the village of Colyttus, get his livelihood? By making cassocks. What makes Menon live so comfortably? His cloak manufacture. And are not most of the inhabitants of Megara in good circumstances enough by the trade which they drive of coats and short jackets?"

"I grant all this," said Aristarchus, "but still there is a difference betwixt these persons and me: for, whereas, they have with them some barbarians whom they have bought, and compel to work what brings them in gain; I, for my part, keep only ladies and gentlemen at my house, persons who are free, and some of them my own relations. Now would you have me to set *them* to work?"

"And because they are free and your relations," said Socrates, "do you think they ought to do nothing but eat and sleep? Do you observe that they, who live thus idle and at their ease, lead more comfortable lives than others? Do you think them more content, more cheerful, that is to say, more happy than those who employ themselves in any of those manufactures we have mentioned, or in whatever else tends to the utility or convenience of life? Do you imagine that idleness and laziness contribute toward our learning things necessary; that they can enable as to retain those things we have already learnt; that they help to strengthen the body or keep it in health; that they can assist us to get riches, or keep what we have got already; and do you believe that labour and industry are good for nothing? Why did your ladies learn what you say they know. Did they believe them to be useless things, and had they resolved never to put them in practice? Or, on the contrary, was it with design to employ themselves in those matters, and to get something by them? Is it a greater piece of wisdom to sit still and do nothing, than to busy oneself in things that are of use in life, and that turn to account? And is it not more reasonable for a man to work than to be with his arms across, thinking how he shall do to live? Shall I tell you my mind, Aristarchus? Well, then, I am of opinion that in the condition you are in you cannot love your guests, nor they you: for this reason, that you, on the one hand, feel they are a burden to you, and they, on the other, perceive you uneasy and discontented on their account. And it is to be feared that the discontent will increase on both sides, and that the sense of past favours will wear off; but when you set them to work you will begin to love them, because they will bring you some profit; and when they find that you regard them with more complacency they will not fail to have more love for you. The remembrance of your kindnesses will be more grateful to them, and the obligations they have to you will be the greater. In a word, you will be kinder relations and better friends. Indeed, if what they were to do was a thing worthy of blame, it would be better to die than to think of it; but what they can do is honourable, and becoming of their sex, and whoever knows how to do a thing well will acquit himself of it with honour and pleasure. Therefore defer no longer to make the proposal to them, since it will be so advantageous to all of you, and be assured they will receive it with joy and pleasure."

"Good God! what a fine scheme you have proposed! Indeed, I cannot but approve of it; nay, it has made such a wonderful impression on my mind, that whereas I was lately against borrowing money at all, because I saw that when I had spent it I should not be in a condition to repay it, I am now resolved to go try where I can take some up upon any terms, to buy tools and other materials to set ourselves to work."

What was proposed was forthwith executed. Aristarchus bought what he wanted; he laid in a provision of wool, and the ladies worked from morning to night. This occupation diverted their melancholy, and, instead of the uneasiness there was before between them and Aristarchus, they began to live in a reciprocal satisfaction. The ladies loved him as their protector, and he considered them as persons who were very useful and necessary to him.

To conclude, some time afterwards Aristarchus came to see Socrates, and related the whole matter to him with great content, and told him the women began to complain that none but he was idle.

"Why do you not put them in mind," said Socrates, "of the fable of the dog? For, in the days when beasts could speak, according to the fable, the sheep said to her master, 'You are a strange man; we yield you wool, lambs, and cheeses, and yet you give us nothing but what we can get upon the ground; and the dog, who brings you in no profit, is kindly used, for you feed him with the same bread you eat yourself.' The dog, overhearing this complaint, answered her: 'It is not without reason that I am used so well. It is I who protect you; it is I who hinder thieves from taking you away, and wolves from sucking your blood. If I were not always keeping watch about you, you would not dare so much as to go to feed.' This answer was the reason that the sheep yielded freely to the dog the honour they pretended to before. In like manner do you also let these ladies know that it is you who are their guardian and protector, and that you watch over them for their safety with as much care as a faithful and courageous dog watcheth over a herd committed to his charge. Tell them that because of you no man dares hurt them, and that it is by your means that they live at ease and in safety."

CHAPTER VIII

SOCRATES PERSUADES EUTHERUS TO ABANDON HIS FORMER WAY OF LIVING, AND TO BETAKE HIMSELF TO SOME MORE USEFUL AND HONOURABLE EMPLOYMENT

ANOTHER time, meeting with Eutherus, one of his old friends, whom he had not seen for a great while before, he inquired of him from whence he came?

"At present," answered Eutherus, "I come not from abroad; but towards the end of the war I returned from a voyage I had made, for, after having lost all the estate I had upon the frontiers, and my father having left me nothing in Attica, I was forced to work for my living, and I believe it better to do so than to be troublesome to others; besides, I can no longer borrow anything, because I have nothing left to mortgage."

"And how much longer," said Socrates, "do you think you shall be able to work for your living?"

"Alas! but a short while," answered Eutherus.

"Nevertheless," replied Socrates, "when you come to be old it will cost you something to maintain yourself, and yet you will not then be able to earn anything."

"You say very true."

"You had best, then," continued Socrates, "employ yourself now in business that will enable you to lay by something for your old age, and get into the service of some rich man, who has occasion for an economist, to have the inspection over his work-men, to gather in his fruits, to preserve what belongs to him, that he may reward you for the service you do him."

"I should find it very difficult," replied Eutherus, "to submit to be a slave."

"Yet," said Socrates, "the magistrates in republics, and all that are in employments, are not, therefore, reputed slaves; on the contrary, they are esteemed honourable."

"Be that as it will," said Eutherus, "I can never think of entering into any office where I might be liable to blame, for I would not like to be censured by another."

"But where," said Socrates, "will you find any employment in which a man is absolutely perfect, and altogether free from blame? For it is very difficult to be so exact as not to fail some-times, and even though we should not have failed, it is hard to escape the censure of bad judges; and I should think it a very odd and surprising thing if in that very employment wherein you say you are now engaged you were so dexterous and expert as that no man should find anything amiss.

"What you are, therefore, to observe is to avoid those who make it their business to find fault without reason, and to have to do with more equitable persons; to undertake what you can actually perform, to reject what you find yourself unfit to do; and when you have taken in hand to do anything, to accomplish it in a man-ner the most excellent and perfect you can. Thus you will be less subject to be blamed, will find relief to your poverty, lead an easier life, be out of danger, and will sufficiently provide for the necessi-ties of your old age."

CHAPTER IX

IN WHAT MANNER SOCRATES TAUGHT HIS FRIEND CRITO TO RID HIMSELF OF SOME INFORMERS, WHO TOOK THE ADVANTAGE OF HIS EASY TEMPER

ONE day Crito, happening to meet Socrates, complained to him that it was very difficult for a man who would keep what he had to live in Athens; "for," said he, "I am now sued by some men, though I never did them the least injury, but only because they know that I had rather give them a little money than embroil myself in the troubles of law."

Socrates said to him, "Do you keep dogs to hinder the wolves from coming at your flocks?"

"You need not doubt but I do," answered Crito.

"Ought you not likewise," replied Socrates, "to keep a man who were able to drive away all those that trouble you without cause?"

"I would with all my heart," said Crito, "but that I fear that in the end he, too, would turn against me."

"Why so?" said Socrates; "is it not better to serve a man like you, and to receive favours from him, than to have him for an enemy? You may be certain that there are in this city many men who would think themselves very happy to be honoured with your friendship."

After this they happened to see a certain person name Archedemus, who was a man of very good parts, eloquent, and extremely skilful in the management of affairs; but withal very

poor and in a low condition, for he was not of that sordid disposition to take all he could get, by what means soever; but he was a
lover of justice and of honest men, and abhorred to make rich,
or to raise himself by informing and backbiting; for he held that
nothing was more base than that wretched practice of those mis-
creants called sycophants or informers. Crito cast an eye upon
him, and as often as they brought him any corn, or wine, or oil,
or any other thing from his country-houses, he sent him some of
it; when he offered sacrifices he invited him to the feasts, and
showed him many civilities of the like nature. Archedemus, seeing the doors of that house open to him at all times, and that he
always found so favourable a reception, laid aside all his former
dependences, and trusted himself wholly to Crito; then he made
it his business immediately to inquire into the characters of
those sycophants who had slandered Crito or informed against
him, and found them to be guilty of many crimes, and that they
had a great number of enemies. This encouraged him to take
them to task, and he prosecuted one of them for a crime which
would have subjected him to a corporal punishment, or at least
to a pecuniary mulct. This fellow, who knew his case to be bad,
and that he could not justify himself, employed all sorts of stratagems to get rid of Archedemus, who nevertheless would not quit
his hold till the other had discharged Crito, and given him
money besides, in name of trouble and charges. He managed
several of his affairs with like success, which made Crito be
thought happy in having him; and as when a shepherd has an
excellent dog, the other shepherds are glad to bring their flocks
near his that they may be safe likewise, so several of Crito's
friends began to make their court to him, and begged him to
lend them Archedemus to defend them. He, for his part, was
glad to oblige Crito; and it was observed at length that not only
Crito lived undisturbed, but all his friends likewise; and if any
one reproached Archedemus that self-interest had made him his
master's creature, and to adore him and be so faithful and zeal-
ous in his service he would answer him thus: — "Which of the two

do you think most dishonourable — to do services to men of quality from whom we have received favours, and to enter into their friendship to declare war against bad men, or to endeavour to prejudice men of honour, and to make them our enemies, that bad men may be our friends?" From thenceforward Crito contracted a strict friendship with Archedemus, and all his friends had likewise a great respect for him.

CHAPTER X

SOCRATES ADVISES DIODORUS TO DO JUSTICE TO THE MERIT OF HERMOGENES, AND TO ACCEPT OF HIS SERVICE AND FRIENDSHIP

SOCRATES, meeting one day with Diodorus, addressed him thus: — "If one of your slaves ran away, would you give yourself any trouble to find him?"

"Yes, certainly," answered he; "and I would give public notice, and promise a reward to any that brought him to me."

"And if one of them were sick, would you take care of him, and send for physicians to endeavour to save his life?"

"Without doubt I would."

"And if you saw," replied Socrates, "one of your friends — that is to say, a person who renders you a thousand times more service than a slave, reduced to extreme want — ought you not to relieve him? I speak this to you on account of Hermogenes. You very well know he is not ungrateful, and that he would scorn to receive the least favour from you and not return you the like. You know likewise that a great number of slaves are not to be valued like one man who serves willingly, who serves with zeal and affection, and who is not only capable of doing what he is desired, but who can likewise of himself think of many things that may be of service to us; who reasons well, who foresees what may happen, and from whom we may expect to receive good advice. Now, the best managers hold it as a maxim that when we find anything of value to be sold cheap we ought to buy it. Think of it, therefore, for as times now go you may procure yourself many friends at a cheap rate."

"You say right," replied Diodorus, "and therefore pray send Hermogenes to me."

"Excuse me in that," answered Socrates, "you would do as well to go to him yourself as to send for him."

This discourse was the reason that Diodorus went to Hermogenes, and for a small gratification obliged him to be his friend; after which Hermogenes took particular care to please Diodorus, and sought all opportunities of serving him and of giving him content

BOOK III

CHAPTER I

OF THE QUALIFICATIONS OF A GENERAL

LET us now see how Socrates was serviceable to those who were desirous to qualify themselves for employments of trust and honour, by advising them to apply themselves diligently to the study of their duty, that they might acquire a perfect knowledge of it.

Having heard that there was arrived at Athens one Dionysodorus, who undertook to teach the art of war, he made the following discourse to one of his friends, who pretended to one of the highest posts in the army:—

"It were a scandalous thing," said Socrates to him, "for a man who aims to be chief over others, to neglect to learn how to command, when so fair an opportunity offers; nay, I think he would rather deserve to be punished, than the man who should undertake to make a statue without having learnt the sculptor's trade; for as in war the whole fortune of the Republic is trusted to the general, it is to be presumed that his good conduct will procure success, and that his faults will be followed with great losses. And, therefore, a man who should neglect to make himself capable of such an employment, and yet pretend to it, ought to be severely punished." By these reasons he persuaded this young man to get himself instructed.

After the youth had imagined that he had acquired some knowledge of the art, he returned to pay Socrates a visit, who, jesting him, addressed the company that were present in this manner:—"Do not you think, gentlemen, that as Homer, when speaking of Agamemnon, gives him the surname of venerable, we ought also to bestow the same epithet on this young man, who justly deserveth to be called by that name, since, like him, he has learned how to command? For, as a man who can play on the lute is a player on that instrument, though he never toucheth it; and as he who is knowing in the art of physic is a physician, though he never practise; so this young man, having learned to command is become a general, though not a man of us should ever give our voice to make him so. On the contrary, it is in vain for him who knows not how to command, to get himself chosen; he will not be one jot a better general for it, no more than he who knows nothing of physic is a better physician, because he has the reputation of being one." Then turning towards the young man, he went on:—"But because it may happen that one of us may have the honour of commanding a regiment or a company in the troops that are to compose your army, to the end we may not be entirely ignorant of the military art, pray tell us by what he began to instruct you."

"By what he ended," answered the young man; "for he showed me only the order that ought to be observed in an army, either in marching, encamping, or fighting."

"But what is that," said Socrates, "in comparison of the many other duties incumbent on a general? He must, besides, take care for the preparations of war; he must furnish the soldiers with necessary ammunition and provisions; he must be inventive, laborious, diligent, patient, quick of apprehension; he must be mild and rigorous together; he must be open and close; he must know to preserve his own, and take what is another's; he must be prodigal and a ravager; he must be liberal and covetous; he must be wary, and yet enterprising. I confess that he ought to know likewise how to draw up his troops in order of battle; and, indeed, order and discipline are the most important things in an army, and without them it is impossible to have any other service of the troops than of a confused heap of stones, bricks, timber, and tiles; but when everything is in its due place, as in a building, when the foundations and the covering are made of materials that will not grow rotten, and which no wet can damage, such as are stones and tiles, and when the bricks and timber are employed in their due places in the body of the edifice, they altogether make a house, which we value among our most considerable enjoyments." Here the young man, interrupting him, said:—

"This comparison puts me in mind of another thing that generals ought to observe; which is, to place their best soldiers in the first and last ranks, and the others in the middle; that those in the first rank may draw them on, and those in the last push them forward."

"He has taught you too," said Socrates, "how to know the good and the bad soldiers asunder, otherwise this rule can be of no use to you; for if you were to reckon money upon a table, and were ordered to lay the best at the two ends, and the worst in the middle, how could you do this, if you had not been shown how to distinguish between the good and the bad?"

"Indeed," replied the young man, "he did not teach me what you mention; and, I suppose, we must learn of ourselves to discern the good soldiers from the bad."

"If you please," continued Socrates, "let us consider how a general ought to govern himself in this matter. If it were to take any money, ought he not to make the most covetous march in the front? If it were an action of great peril, ought he not to send the most ambitious, because they are the men who, out of a desire of glory, rush into the midst of dangers? And as for them, you would not be much troubled to know them, for they are forward enough in discovering themselves. But tell me, when this master showed you the different ways of ordering an army, did he teach you when to make use of one way, and when of another?"

"Not at all," answered he.

"And yet," replied Socrates, "the same order is not always to be observed, nor the same commands given, but to be changed according to the different occasions."

"He taught me nothing of that," said the young man.

"Go to him, then," added Socrates, "and ask him concerning it; for if he know anything of the matter, and have ever so little honour, he will be ashamed to have taken your money and send you away so ill-instructed."

CHAPTER II

THE CHARACTER OF A GOOD PRINCE

ANOTHER time he asked a general, whom the Athenians had lately chosen, why Homer calls Agamemnon the pastor of the people? "Is it not," said he, "because as a shepherd ought to take care of his flocks, that they be well and want for nothing; so a general ought to take care to keep his soldiers always in a good condition, to see they be supplied with provisions, and to bring to a happy issue the design that made them take arms, which is to overcome their enemies, and to live more happily afterwards? And why does the same poet praise Agamemnon likewise for being —

'At once a gracious prince and generous warrior'?

For is it not true, that to gain a prince the character of being generous and a warrior too, it is not sufficient to be brave in his own person, and to fight with intrepidity; but he must likewise animate the whole army, and be the cause that every soldier behave himself like him? and to gain the reputation of a good and gracious prince, it is not enough to have secured his private affairs, he must also take care that plenty and happiness be seen in all places of his dominions. For kings are not chosen to take care of themselves only, but to render happy the people who choose them. All people engage in war only to secure their own quiet, and choose commanders that they may have guides to conduct them to the end which they propose to themselves. A general, therefore, ought to prepare the way of good fortune to those who raise him to that dignity; this is the most glorious success he can desire, as nothing can be more ignominious to him than to do the contrary."

We see by this discourse that Socrates, designing to give the idea of a good prince, required scarce anything of him but to render his subjects happy.

CHAPTER III

ON THE BUSINESS OF A
GENERAL OF HORSE

SOCRATES at another time, as I well remember, had the following
conference with a general of the cavalry: —

"What was your reason," said Socrates, "to desire this office? I
cannot think it was that you might march first at the head of the
troops, for the horse-archers are to march before you. Nor can I
believe it was to make yourself be known, for no men are more
generally known than madmen. Perhaps it was because you
thought you could mend what was amiss in the cavalry, and make
the troops better than they are, to the end that if the Republic
should have occasion to use them, you might be able to do your
country some eminent service."

"That is my design," answered the other.

"It were well you could do this," said Socrates, "but does not
your office oblige you to have an eye on the horses and troopers?"

"Most certainly."

"What course will you then take," continued Socrates, "to
get good horses?"

"It is not my business to look to that," replied the general;
"every trooper must take care for himself."

"And what," said Socrates, "if they bring you horses whose feet
and legs are good for nothing, or that are so weak and lean that
they cannot keep up with the others, or so restive and vicious that

it would be impossible to make them keep their ranks, what good could you expect from such cavalry? What service would you be able to do the State?"

"You are much in the right, Socrates, and I promise you I will take care what horses are in my troops.'

"And will you not have an eye likewise on the troopers?"

"Yes," answered he. "In my opinion then," answered Socrates, "the first thing you ought to do is to make them learn to get a horseback."

"No doubt of it," replied the general, "for by that means they would the more easily escape, if they should happen to be thrown off their horses."

Socrates went on: "You ought also to make them exercise, sometimes here, sometimes there, and particularly in places like those where the enemy generally is, that they may be good horsemen in all sorts of countries; for when you are to fight you will not send to bid the enemy come to you in the plain, where you used to exercise your horse. You must train them up, likewise, to lance the spear; and if you would make them very brave fellows, you must inspire them with a principle of honour, and inflame them with rage against the enemy."

"Fear not," said he, "that I will spare my labour."

"But have you," resumed Socrates, "thought on the means to make yourself obeyed? for without that all your brave troopers will avail you nothing."

"It is true," said he, "but how shall I gain that point of them?"

"Know you not," said Socrates, "that in all things men readily obey those whom they believe most capable? Thus in our sickness we most willingly submit to the prescriptions of the best physicians; at sea, to the most skilful pilot; and in affairs of agriculture, to him who has most experience in it."

"All this I grant you."

"It is then to be presumed, that in the conduct of the cavalry he who makes it appear that he understands it best will be the person whom the others will be best pleased to obey."

"But if I let them see that I am most worthy to command, will that be sufficient to make them obey me?"

"Yes, certainly," said Socrates, "if you can persuade them besides that their honour and safety depend on that obedience."

"And how shall I be able to make them sensible of this?"

"With less trouble," answered Socrates, "than it would be to prove that it is better to be virtuous than vicious."

"Then a general," added the other, "ought to study the art of speaking well?"

"Do you imagine," said Socrates, "that he will be able to execute his office without speaking a word? It is by speech that we know what the laws command us to learn for the conduct of our lives. No excellent knowledge can be attained without the use of speech; the best method to instruct is by discourse, and they who are thoroughly versed in the sciences speak with the applause of all the world. But have you observed," continued he, "that in all sorts of occasions the Athenians distinguish themselves above all the Greeks, and that no Republic can show such youths as that of Athens? For example: when we send from hence a choir of musicians to the Temple of Apollo in the Isle of Delos, it is certain that none comparable to them are sent from other cities; not that the Athenians have better voices than the others, nor that their bodies are more robust and better made, but the reason is because they are more fond of honour, and this desire of honour is what excites men to excellent actions. Do not you think, therefore, that if good care were taken of our cavalry, it would excel that of other nations, in the beauty of arms and horses, in order of good discipline, and in bravery in fight; provided the Athenians were persuaded that this would be a means to acquire them glory and renown?"

"I am of your opinion."

"Go, then, and take care of your troops," said Socrates, "make them serviceable to you, that you may be so to the Republic."

"Your advice is good," said he, "and I will immediately follow it."

CHAPTER IV

A DISCOURSE OF SOCRATES WITH NICOMACHIDES, IN WHICH HE SHOWETH THAT A MAN SKILFUL IN HIS OWN PROPER BUSINESS, AND WHO MANAGES HIS AFFAIRS WITH PRUDENCE AND SAGACITY, MAY MAKE, WHEN OCCASION OFFERS, A GOOD GENERAL

ANOTHER time, Socrates meeting Nicomachides, who was coming from the assembly where they had chosen the magistrates, asked him, "of whom they had made choice to command the army?"

Nicomachides answered: "Alas! the Athenians would not chose me; me! who have spent all my life in arms, and have gone through all the degrees of a soldier; who have been first a private sentinel, then a captain, next a colonel of horse, and who am covered all over with wounds that I have received in battles" (at these words he bared his breast, and showed the large scars which were remaining in several places of his body); "but they have chosen Antisthenes, who has never served in the infantry, who even in the cavalry never did anything remarkable, and whose only talent consists in knowing how to get money."

"So much the better," said Socrates, "for then the army will be well paid."

"A merchant," replied Nicomachides, "knows how to get money as well as he; and does it follow from thence that he is fit to be a general?"

"You take no notice," replied Socrates, "that Antisthenes is fond of honour, and desirous to excel all others in whatever he undertakes, which is a very necessary qualification in a general. Have you not observed, that whenever he gave a comedy to the people, he always gained the prize?"

"There is a wide difference," answered Nicomachides, "between commanding an army and giving orders concerning a comedy."

"But," said Socrates, "though Antisthenes understands not music, nor the laws of the stage, yet he found out those who were skilful in both, and by their means succeeded extremely well."

"And when he is at the head of the army," continued Nicomachides, "I suppose you will have him to find out too some to give orders, and some to fight for him?"

"Why not?" replied Socrates, "for if in the affairs of war he take the same care to provide himself with persons skilful in that art, and fit to advise him, as he did in the affair of the plays, I see not what should hinder him from gaining the victory in the former as well as in the latter. And it is very likely that he will be better pleased to expend his treasure to obtain an entire victory over the enemy, which will redound to the honour and interest of the whole Republic, than to be at a great expense for shows, to overcome his citizens in magnificence, and to gain a victory, which can be honourable to none but himself and those of his tribe."

"We must then infer," said Nicomachides, "that a man who knows well how to give a comedy knows well how to command an army?"

"Let us rather conclude," answered Socrates, "that every man who has judgment enough to know the things that are necessary for his designs, and can procure them, can never fail of success, whether he concern himself with the stage, or govern a State, or command an army, or manage a family."

"Indeed," resumed Nicomachides, "I could never have thought you would have told me, too, that a good economist would make a good general."

"Come, then," said Socrates, "let us examine wherein consists the duty of the one and of the other, and see what relation there is between those two conditions. Must not both of them keep those that are under them in submission and obedience?"

"I grant it."

"Must not both of them take care to employ every one in the business he is fit for? Must he not punish those who do amiss and reward those that do well? Must they not make themselves be esteemed by those they command? Ought they not alike to strengthen themselves with friends to assist them upon occasion? Ought they not to know how to preserve what belongs to them, and to be diligent and indefatigable in the performance of their duty?"

"I own," answered Nicomachides, "that all you have said concerns them equally; but if they were to fight it would not be the same as to both of them."

"Why?" said Socrates. "Have not both of them enemies?"

"They have."

"And would it not be the advantage of both to get the better of them?"

"I allow it," said Nicomachides; "but what will economy be good for when they are to come to blows?"

"It is then it will be most necessary," replied Socrates. "For when the good economist sees that the greatest profit he can get is to overcome, and that the greatest loss he can suffer is to be beaten, he will prepare himself with all the advantages that can procure him the victory, and will carefully avoid whatever might be the cause of his defeat. Thus, when he sees his army well provided with all things, and in a condition that seems to promise a good success, he will give his enemies battle; but when he wants anything he will avoid coming to an engagement with them. Thus you see how economy may be of use to him; and therefore, Nicomachides, despise not those who apply themselves to it; for between the conduct of a family and that of a State the sole difference is that of a greater or lesser number; for as to all besides there is much conformity between them. The sum of what I have advanced is this, that without men there could not be any policy or any economy, that they are often executed by the same persons, and that they who are called to the government of the Republic are the very same whom great men employ for their private affairs. Lastly, that they who make use of proper persons for their several businesses are successful in their economy and in politics; and that, on the contrary, they who fail in this point commit great faults both in one and the other."

CHAPTER V

A CONVERSATION BETWEEN SOCRATES
AND PERICLES CONCERNING THE THEN
PRESENT STATE OF THE REPUBLIC OF
ATHENS, IN WHICH SOCRATES LAYS DOWN
A METHOD BY WHICH THE ATHENIANS
MAY RECOVER THEIR ANCIENT
LUSTRE AND REPUTATION

SOCRATES one day being in company with Pericles, the son of the great Pericles, introduced the following discourse:—

"I hope that when you command the army the Republic will be more successful and gain more glory in their wars than formerly."

"I should be glad of it," answered Pericles, "but I see little likelihood of it."

"We may bring this matter to the test," said Socrates. "Is it not true that the Bœotians are not more numerous than the Athenians?"

"I know it."

"Nor are they either braver or stronger?"

"True, they are not."

"Do you believe that they agree better among themselves?"

"Quite the contrary," said Pericles; "for there is a great misunderstanding between most of the Bœotians and the Thebans, because of the great hardships the latter put upon the former, and we have nothing of this among us."

"But the Bœotians," replied Socrates, "are wonderfully ambitious and obliging; and these are the qualities that naturally push men on to expose themselves for the sake of glory and of their country."

"The Athenians," answered Pericles, "come not short of them in either of those qualities."

"It is true," replied Socrates, "that there is no nation whose ancestors have done braver actions, and in greater number, than those of the Athenians. And these domestic examples excite us to courage, and create in us a true love of virtue and bravery."

"Notwithstanding all this," continued Pericles, "you see that after the defeat of Tolmides at Lebadia, where we lost a thousand men, and after another misfortune that happened to Hippocrates before Delium, the greatness of the Athenians is sunk so low, and the courage of the Bœotians so increased, that they, who even in their own country durst not look the Athenians in the face without the assistance of the Lacedemonians and of the other States of the Peloponnesus, now threaten Attica with their single forces. And that the Athenians, who before ravaged Bœotia when it was not defended by foreign troops, begin to fear, in their turn, that the Bœotians will put Attica to fire and sword."

"In my opinion," answered Socrates, "a governor ought to be well pleased to find a republic in such a condition; for fear makes a people more careful, more obedient, and more submissive. Whereas a too great security is attended with carelessness, luxury, and disobedience. This is plainly seen in men who are at sea. When they fear not anything, there is nothing in the ship but confusion and disorder; but when they apprehend that they shall be attacked by pirates, or that a tempest is hanging over their head, they not only do whatever they are commanded, but even observe a profound silence, waiting the order of their captain, and are as decent and orderly in their behaviour and motions as those who dance at a public entertainment."

"We shall yield, then," replied Pericles, "that the Athenians are obedient. But how shall we do to create in them an emulation to imitate the virtue of their ancestors to equal their reputation and to restore the happiness of their age in this present one?"

"If we would have them," answered Socrates, "make themselves masters of an estate, which is in the possession of others, we need only tell them that it is descended to them from their forefathers, and they will immediately be for having it again. If we would encourage them to take the first rank among the virtuous, we must persuade them that it is their due from all antiquity, and that if they will take care to preserve to themselves this advantage they will infallibly likewise surpass others in power. We must frequently represent to them that the most ancient of their predecessors were highly esteemed on account of their great virtue."

"You would be understood," said Pericles, "to speak of the contention of two of the divinities concerning the patronage of the city of Athens, of which the citizens, in the days of Cecrops, were chosen arbitrators on account of their virtue."

"You are in the right," said Socrates; "but I would have them be put in mind likewise of the birth and nourishment of Erictheus, and of the war that was in his time against the neighbouring nations; as also of that which was made in favour of the descendants of Hercules against the people of Peloponnesus, and, in short, of all the other wars that were in the days of Theseus, in which our ancestors were always reputed the most valiant men of their age. If you think fit, they may likewise be told what the descendants of these ancients and our predecessors of the last age have done. They may be represented to them as resisting sometimes with their own forces only the nations whom all Asia obeyed, whose dominions extended into Europe as far as Macedonia, and who had inherited a potent empire from their fathers, together with formidable forces, and who were already renowned for many great exploits. Sometimes you mast relate to them the victories they gained by sea and land in conjunction with the Lacedemonians, who are likewise reputed a very brave people.

They should be told also that great commotions being arisen among the Greeks, and the most part of them having changed their places of abode, the Athenians always continued in their country; that they have been chosen by several people to arbitrate their differences, and that the oppressed have always fled to them for protection."

"When I reflect on all this," said Pericles, "I am surprised to see the Republic so much fallen off from what it was."

"In my opinion," replied Socrates, "she has behaved herself like those persons who, for having too great advantage over their rivals, begin to neglect themselves, and grow in the end pusillanimous; for after the Athenians saw themselves raised above the other Greeks they indulged themselves in indolence, and became at length degenerate."

"What course must they take now," said Pericles "to regain the lustre of their ancient virtue?"

"They need only call to mind," replied Socrates, "what were the exercises and the discipline of their ancestors, and if, like them, they apply themselves to those practices, they will no doubt arrive at their perfection; or if they will not govern themselves by that example, let them imitate the nations that are now uppermost; let them observe the same conduct, follow the same customs, and be assured they will equal, if not surpass them, if they labour to do so."

"You seem to be of opinion, my dear Socrates, that virtue is much estranged from our Republic? And, indeed, when will the Athenians respect old age as they of Sparta do, since they begin, even by their own fathers, to deride men advanced in years? When, too, will they use themselves to the manly exercises of that Republic, since they not only neglect the good disposition and activity of body, but laugh at those who endeavour to acquire them? When will they be obedient to the magistrates, they who make it a glory to despise them? When will they be in perfect unity, they who, instead of assisting, daily prejudice one another, and who envy one another more than they do all the rest of mankind? They are every day quarrelling in the public and private assemblies; they are every day suing one another, and had rather find their own advantage in the ruin of their neighbours than get an honest gain by reciprocally assisting one another. The magistrates mind not the Government of the Republic any farther than their own interests are concerned, and, therefore, they use their utmost endeavours to be in office and authority; and for this reason in the administration of the State there is so much ignorance and malice, and such animosities, and so many different parties among private persons. And I much fear that this mischief will get such a head that at length there will be no remedy against it, and that the Republic will sink under the weight of its misfortunes."

"Fear it not," said Socrates, "and do not believe that the Athenians labour under an incurable disease. Do you not observe how skilful and obedient they are at sea, that in the combats for prizes they exactly obey the orders of those that preside there, and in the comedies how readily they comply with what they are bid to do?"

"I see it well," answered Pericles, "and cannot but wonder that they are so ready to obey in these and the like occasions, and that the military men, who ought to be the chosen part of the citizens, are so mutinous and refractory."

"And what say you," pursued Socrates, "to the Senate of the Areopagus; are they not all of them persons of great worth? Do you know any judges who discharge their office with more integrity, and who more exactly observe the laws, who more faithfully render justice to private men, and who more worthily acquit themselves of all manner of affairs?"

"I blame them not," said Pericles.

"Despair not, then, of the Athenians," added Socrates, "as of an untractable people."

"But it is in war," replied Pericles, "that much discipline is required, and much modesty and obedience, and these things the Athenians wholly want in that occasion."

"Perhaps, too," continued Socrates, "they who command them know little of their own duty. Do you not take notice that no man undertakes to govern a company of musicians, or of comedians, or of dancers, or of wrestlers, unless he be capable of it; and that all who take such employments upon them can give an account where they have learnt the exercises of which they are become masters? Our misfortunes in war, then, I very much apprehend, must be owing in a great measure to the bad education of our generals.

"I know very well that you are not of this number, and that you have improved to your advantage the time you have spent in learning the art of war and other laudable exercises. I imagine, likewise, that in the memoirs of your father, the great Pericles, you have found many rare stratagems, and that by your diligence you have also collected up and down a great number of others. Nor do I doubt but that you frequently meditate on these matters, that nothing may be wanting in you that may be of use to a general. Insomuch, that if you find yourself in doubt of anything, you immediately have recourse to those that know it, and spare neither presents nor civilities to incline them to assist you and to teach you the things of which you are ignorant."

"Alas! Socrates," said Pericles, "you flatter me, and flatter me for many things that, I am afraid, I am deficient in; but by that you instruct me in my duty."

Upon this Socrates, interrupting him—"I will," said he, "give you an advice. Have you not observed that in the high mountains, which are the frontiers of Attica, and divide it from Bœotia, the roads through which you must of necessity pass to go from one country to the other are very rough and narrow?"

"Yes, I have."

"Tell me, besides, have you never heard say that the Mysians and the Pisidians, who are in possession of advantageous places where they dwell in the dominions of the King of Persia, arm themselves lightly, and make continual inroads upon the neighbouring provinces, and by that means are very troublesome to that king's subjects, and preserve their own liberty?"

"I have heard so."

"It is probable, too," continued Socrates, "that if the Athenians would possess themselves of the mountains that are between Bœotia and Attica, and if they took care to send thither some young men with arms proper for in-roaders, our enemies would be much prejudiced by them, and all those mountains would be as a great rampart to cover our country from their insults."

"I believe what you say," answered Pericles, "and take all the advices you have given me to be very good."

"If you think them so," replied Socrates, "endeavour, my friend, to put them in practice; for if any of them succeed you will receive the honour, and the Republic the profit; and even though they should not meet with success the Republic would have no inconvenience to apprehend, nor you the least dishonour."

CHAPTER VI

SOCRATES DISSUADES GLAUCON, A VERY FORWARD YOUTH, FROM TAKING UPON HIM THE GOVERNMENT OF THE REPUBLIC, FOR WHICH HE WAS UNFIT

A young man whose name was Glaucon, the son of Ariston, had so fixed it in his head to govern the Republic, that before he was twenty years of age he frequently presented himself before the people to discourse of affairs of state; nor was it in the power of his relations or friends to dissuade him from that design, though all the world laughed at him for it, and though sometimes he was dragged from the tribunal by force. Socrates had a kindness for him, upon account of Plato and Charmidas, and he only it was who made him change his resolution. He met him, and accosted him in so winning a manner, that he first obliged him to hearken to his discourse. He began with him thus: —

"You have a mind, then, to govern the Republic, my friend?"

"I have so," answered Glaucon.

"You cannot," replied Socrates, "have a more noble design; for if you can accomplish it you will be absolute. You will be able to serve your friends, you will raise your family, you will extend the bounds of your country, you will be known not only in Athens but through all Greece, and perhaps your renown will fly even to the barbarous nations, as did that of Themistocles. In short, wherever you come you will be respected and admired."

These words soothed up Glaucon, and won him to give ear to Socrates, who went on in this manner: — "But it is certain, my dear friend, that if you desire to be honoured, you must be useful to the State."

"Certainly," said Glaucon.

"I conjure you, then, to tell me," replied Socrates, "what is the first service that you desire to render the State?" Glaucon was considering what to answer, when Socrates continued: — "If you intended to make the fortune of one of your friends, you would endeavour to make him rich, and thus perhaps you will make it your business to enrich the Republic."

"I would," answered Glaucon.

"Would not the way to enrich the Republic," replied Socrates, "be to increase its revenue?"

"It is very likely it would," said Glaucon.

"Tell me, then, in what consists the revenue of the State, and to how much it may amount? I presume you have particularly studied this matter, to the end that if anything should be lost on one hand, you might know where to make it good on another, and that if a fund should fail on a sudden, you might immediately be able to settle another in its place."

"I protest," answered Glaucon, "I have never thought of this."

"Tell me at least the expenses of the Republic, for no doubt you intend to retrench the superfluous."

"I never thought of this neither," said Glaucon.

"You had best, then, put off to another time your design of enriching the Republic, which you can never be able to do while you are ignorant both of its expense and revenue."

"There is another way to enrich a State," said Glaucon, "of which you take no notice, and that is by the ruin of its enemies."

"You are in the right," answered Socrates; "but to this end it is necessary to be stronger than they, otherwise we should run the hazard of losing what we have. He, therefore, who talks of undertaking a war, ought to know the strength on both sides, to the end that if his party be the stronger, he may boldly advise for war, and that if it be the weaker, he may dissuade the people from engaging themselves in so dangerous an enterprise."

"All this is true."

"Tell me, then," continued Socrates, "how strong our forces are by sea and land, and how strong are our enemies?"

"Indeed," said Glaucon, "I cannot tell you that on a sudden."

"If you have a list of them in writing, pray show it me, I should be glad to hear it read."

"I never took a list of them."

"I see, then," said Socrates, "that we shall not engage in war so soon; for it is like that the greatness of the undertaking will hinder you from maturely weighing all the consequences of it in the beginning of your government. But," continued he, "you have thought of the defence of the country, you know what garrisons are necessary, and what are not; you know what number of troops is sufficient in one garrison, and not sufficient in another; you will cause the necessary garrisons to be reinforced, and will disband those that are useless?"

"I should be of opinion," said Glaucon, "to leave none of them on foot, because they ruin a country, on pretence of defending it."

"But," Socrates objected, "if all the garrisons were taken away, there would be nothing to hinder the first comer from carrying off what he pleased. But how come you to know that the garrisons behave themselves so ill? Have you been upon the place, have you seen them?"

"Not at all; but I suspect it to be so."

"When, therefore, we are certain of it," said Socrates, "and can speak upon better grounds than simple conjectures, we will propose this advice to the Senate."

"It will be very proper to do so," said Glaucon.

"It comes into my mind too," continued Socrates, "that you have never been at the mines of silver, to examine why they bring not in so much now as they did formerly."

"You say true, I have never been there."

"Indeed, they say the place is very unhealthy, and that may excuse you."

"You rally me now," said Glaucon.

Socrates added, "But I believe you have at least observed how much corn our lands produce, how long it will serve to supply our city, and how much more we shall want for the whole year, to the end you may not be surprised with a scarcity of bread, but may give timely orders for the necessary provisions."

"There is a deal to do," said Glaucon, "if we must take care of all these things."

"There is so," replied Socrates; "and it is even impossible to manage our own families well unless we know all that is wanting, and take care to provide it. As you see, therefore, that our city is composed of above ten thousand families, and it being a difficult task to watch over them all at once, why did you not first try to retrieve your uncle's affairs, which are running to decay, that after having given a proof of your care, faithfulness, and capacity in that smaller trust, you might have taken upon you a greater? But now, when you find yourself incapable of aiding a private man, how can you think of behaving yourself so as to be useful to a whole people? Ought a man who has not strength enough to carry a hundred pound weight undertake to carry a burden that is much heavier?"

"I would have done good service to my uncle," said Glaucon, "if he would have taken my advice."

"How!" replied Socrates; "have you hitherto been unable to govern your uncle, who is but one person, and do you imagine, when you have failed in that, to govern the whole Athenians, whose minds are so fickle and inconstant? Take heed, my dear Glaucon, take heed, lest a too great desire of glory should render you despised. Consider how dangerous it is to speak and employ ourselves about things we do not understand. What a figure do those forward and rash people make in the world who do so: and you yourself may judge whether they acquire more esteem than blame, whether they are more admired than contemned. Think, on the contrary, with how much honour a man is regarded who understands perfectly what he says and what he does, and then you will confess that renown and applause have always been the recompense of true merit, and shame the reward of ignorance and temerity. If, therefore, you would be honoured endeavour to be a man of true merit, for if you enter upon the government of the Republic with a mind more sagacious than usual, I shall not wonder if you succeed in all your designs."

CHAPTER VII

SOCRATES PERSUADETH CHARMIDAS, A PERSON OF MERIT AND GREAT CAPACITY, BUT VERY MODEST AND DIFFIDENT OF HIMSELF, TO UNDERTAKE THE GOVERN-MENT OF THE REPUBLIC

As Socrates, who was ever watchful for the interests of his country, and consulted the good of every one with whom he conversed, took care, on the one hand, to dissuade persons who had no capacity for it, however bent they were upon the thing, from entering upon any offices of trust, so he was ever mindful, on the other, to persuade those that were bashful and diffident to take upon themselves the government of the Republic, provided he knew they had proper talents and abilities for it. In confirmation whereof we shall here relate a conversation of his with Charmidas, the son of Glaucon. Socrates, who knew him to be a man of sense and merit, and more capable to govern the Republic than any that were then in that post, but withal a person very diffident of himself—one that dreaded the people, and was mightily averse from engaging himself in public business—addressed himself to him in this manner:—

"Tell me, Charmidas, if you knew any man who could gain the prizes in the public games, and by that means render himself illustrious, and acquire glory to his country, what would you say of him if he refused to offer himself to the combat?"

"I would say," answered Charmidas, "that he was a mean-spirited, effeminate fellow."

"And if a man were capable of governing a Republic, of increasing its power by his advices, and of raising himself by this means to a high degree of honour, would you not brand him likewise with meanness of soul if he would not present himself to be employed?"

"Perhaps I might," said Charmidas; "but why do you ask me this question?"

"Because you are capable," replied Socrates, "of managing the affairs of the Republic, and yet you avoid doing so, though in the quality of a citizen you are obliged to take care of the commonwealth."

"And wherein have you observed this capacity in me?"

"When I have seen you in conversation with the Ministers of State," answered Socrates; "for if they impart any affairs to you, I see you give them good advice, and when they commit any errors you make them judicious remonstrances."

"But there is a very great difference, my dear Socrates," replied Charmidas, "between discoursing in private and contending in a public manner before the people."

"And yet," replied Socrates, "a skilful arithmetician can calculate as well in presence of several persons as when alone; and they who can play well upon the lute in their closets play likewise well in company."

"But you know," said Charmidas, "that fear and shame, which are so natural to man, affect us more in public assemblies than in private companies."

"Is it possible," said Socrates, "that you can converse so unconcernedly with men of parts and authority, and that you should not have assurance enough to speak to fools? Are you afraid to present yourself before dyers, shoemakers, masons, smiths, labourers, and brokers? for of such are composed the popular assemblies. This is the same thing as to be the most expert in a fencing-school, and to fear the thrust of an unskilful person who never handled a foil. Thus you, though you speak boldly in the presence of the chief men of the Republic, among whom there might perhaps be found some who would despise you, dare not, nevertheless, speak in the presence of an illiterate multitude, who know nothing of the affairs of state, and who are not capable of despising you, and you fear to be laughed at by them."

"Do they not usually," said Charmidas, "laugh at those who speak best?"

"So likewise," said Socrates, "do the men of quality with whom you converse every day; and I am surprised that you have eloquence and persuasive sense sufficient to bring these to reason, and that you think not yourself capable even to approach the others. Learn to know yourself better, Charmidas, and take care not to fall into a fault that is almost general; for all men inquire curiously enough into the affairs of others, but they never enter into their own bosoms to examine themselves as they ought.

"Be no longer, then, thus negligent in this matter, consider yourself with more attention, and let not slip the occasions of serving the Republic, and of rendering it, if possible, more flourishing than it is. This will be a blessing, whose influence will descend not only on the other citizens, but on your best friends and yourself."

CHAPTER VIII

SOCRATES' DISPUTE WITH ARISTIPPUS CONCERNING THE GOOD AND BEAUTIFUL

ONE day Aristippus proposed a captious question to Socrates, meaning to surprise him; and this by way of revenge, for his having before put him to a stand: but Socrates answered him warily, and as a person who has no other design in his conversations than the improvement of his hearers.

The question which Aristippus asked him was whether he knew in the world any good thing, and if Socrates had answered him that meat, or drink, or riches, or health, or strength, or courage are good things, he would forthwith have shown him that it may happen that they are very bad. He therefore gave him such an answer as he ought; and because he knew very well that when we feel any indisposition we earnestly desire to find a remedy for it, he said to him: "Do you ask me, for example, whether I know anything that is good for a fever?"

"No," said Aristippus.

"Or for sore eyes?" said Socrates.

"Neither."

"Do you mean anything that is good against hunger?"

"Not in the least," answered Aristippus.

"I promise you," said Socrates, "that if you ask me for a good thing that is good for nothing, I know no such thing, nor have anything to do with it."

Aristippus pressed him yet further, and asked him whether he knew any beautiful thing. "I know a great many," said Socrates.

"Are they all like one another?" continued Aristippus.

"Not in the least," answered Socrates, "for they are very different from one another."

"And how is it possible that two beautiful things should be contrary one to the other?"

"This," said Socrates, "is seen every day in men: a beautiful make and disposition of body for running is very different from a beautiful make and disposition for wrestling: the excellence and beauty of a buckler is to cover well him that wears it. On the contrary, the excellence and beauty of a dart is to be light and piercing."

"You answer me," said Aristippus, "as you answered me before, when I asked you whether you knew any good thing."

"And do you think," replied Socrates, "that the good and the beautiful are different? Know you not that the things that are beautiful are good likewise in the same sense? It would be false to say of virtue that in certain occasions it is beautiful, and in others good. When we speak of men of honour we join the two qualities, and call them excellent and good. In our bodies beauty and goodness relate always to the same end. In a word, all things that are of any use in the world are esteemed beautiful and good, with regard to the subject for which they are proper."

"At this rate you might find beauty in a basket to carry dung," said Aristippus.

"Yes, if it be well made for that use," answered Socrates; "and, on the contrary, I would say that a buckler of gold was ugly if it was ill-made."

"Would you say," pursued Aristippus, "that the same thing may be beautiful and ugly at once?"

"I would say that it might be good and bad. Often what is good for hunger is bad for a fever; and what is good for a fever is very bad for hunger; often what is beautiful to be done in running is ugly to be done in wrestling; and what is beautiful to do in wrestling is ugly in running. For all things are reputed beautiful and good when they are compared with those which they suit or become, as they are esteemed ugly and bad when compared with those they do not become."

Thus we see that when Socrates said that beautiful houses were the most convenient, he taught plainly enough in what manner we ought to build them, and he reasoned thus: "Ought not he who builds a house to study chiefly how to make it most pleasant and most convenient?" This proposition being granted, he pursued: "Is it not a pleasure to have a house that is cool in summer and warm in winter? And does not this happen in buildings that front towards the south? For the beams of the sun enter into the apartments in winter, and only pass over the covering in summer. For this reason the houses that front towards the south ought to be very high, that they may receive the sun in winter; and, on the contrary, those that front towards the north ought to be very low, that they may be less exposed to the cold winds of that quarter." In short, he used to say, that he had a very beautiful and very agreeable house, who could live there with ease during all the seasons of the year, and keep there in safety all that he has; but that for painting and other ornaments, there was more trouble in them than pleasure.

He said further that retired places, and such as could be seen from afar, were very proper to erect altars and build temples in; for though we are at a distance from them, yet it is a satisfaction to pray in sight of the holy places, and as they are apart from the haunts of men, innocent souls find more devotion in approaching them.

CHAPTER IX

SOCRATES RETURNS SUITABLE ANSWERS TO A VARIETY OF QUESTIONS PROPOSED TO HIM

ANOTHER time being asked whether courage can be learnt as an art or was a gift of Nature, he answered: "In my opinion, as we see many bodies that are naturally more vigorous than others, and that better endure fatigue, so there are some souls that are naturally more brave, and look dangers in the face with greater resolution. For I see some men, who live under the same laws, who are brought up in the same customs, and who are not all equally valiant. Nevertheless, I believe that education and exercise add much to natural courage. Whence comes it to pass that the Scythians and the Thracians durst not face the Lacedemonians with pikes and targets; and, on the contrary, that the Lacedemonians would not fight against the Thracians with shields and darts, nor against the Scythians with bows? I see it to be the same in all other things, and that when some men are better inclined by nature for certain things than other men are, they very much advance and perfect themselves in those things by study and diligence. This shows that they who are most favoured by Nature, as well as those to whom she has been less indulgent, ought to apply themselves assiduously to the things by which they would gain themselves a reputation."

He allowed no difference between knowledge and temperance; and he held that he who knows what is good and embraces it, who knows what is bad and avoids it, is learned and temperate; and when he was asked whether he believed that they who know very well what ought to be done, but do quite otherwise, were learned and temperate? "On the contrary," answered he, "they are very ignorant and very stupid, for, in my opinion, every man who, in the great number of possible things that offer themselves to him, can discern what is most advantageous for him to do, never fails to do it; but all who govern not themselves well and as they ought, are neither learned nor men of good morals."

He said likewise that justice and every other virtue is only a science, because all the actions of justice and of the other virtues are good and honourable; and that all who know the beauty of these actions think nothing more charming; as, on the contrary, they who are ignorant of them cannot perform any one virtuous action, or, if they attempt to do it, are sure to perform it in a wrong manner. So that the persons only who possess this science can do just and good actions; but all just and good actions are done by the means of virtue, therefore justice and virtue is only a science.

He said, moreover, that folly is contrary to knowledge, and yet he did not allow ignorance to be a folly; but that not to know oneself, or to imagine one knows what he does not know, is a weakness next to folly. And he observed that among the vulgar a man is not accused of folly for being mistaken in things that are unknown to most of the world, but for mistaking in things which no man mistakes that knows anything at all; as if any man should think himself so tall as to be obliged to stoop when he came in at the gates of the city; or if he thought himself so strong as to undertake to carry away whole houses on his back, or to do any other thing visibly impossible, the people would say that he had lost his wits, which they do not say of those who commit only some slight extravagances; and as they give the name of love to a violent affection only, so they give the name of folly only to an extraordinary disorder of the mind.

Reflecting on the nature of envy, he said that it is a certain grief of mind, which proceeds, not from the misfortune of friends or good fortune of enemies, but (which is very surprising) only from the prosperity of friends. "For," said he, "those may be truly said to be envious who cannot endure to see their friends happy." But, some wondering whether it were possible for a man to be grieved at the good fortune of his friend, he justified the truth of what he had advanced, by telling them plainly that there are some men so variously affected towards their friends, that, while they are in calamity and distress, they will compassionate and succour them, but when they are well and in prosperity will fret at and envy them. "But this," he said, "is a fault from which wise and good men are free, and never to be found but in weak and wicked minds."

As to idleness, he said that he had observed that most men were always in action, for they who play at dice, or who serve to make others laugh, are doing something, but in effect they are idle, because they might employ themselves more usefully. To which he added, that no man finds leisure to quit a good employment for an ill one, and that if he did he would deserve the greater blame, in that he wanted not something to do before.

He said likewise that the sceptre makes not the king, and that princes and governors are not they whom chance or the choice of the people has raised to those dignities, nor those who have established themselves in them by fraud or force, but they who know how to command; for if it were allowed that it is the duty of a prince to command, as it is the duty of a subject to obey, he showed in consequence of it that in a ship, where there are several persons, the honour of commanding it is given to him who is most capable of it, and that all obey him, without excepting even the owner of the vessel; that likewise in husbandry, he to whom the land belongs obeys his own servants, if they understand agriculture better than himself; that thus the sick obey the physicians, and they who learn exercises, their masters; nay, that even women are masters of the men in working with the needle, because they understand it better than they; in short, that in all things which require care and industry men govern themselves when they think they are capable of doing so; otherwise, they leave themselves to the conduct of such as they judge to have more capacity, and take care to have them near at hand for that purpose. And if any man made him this objection, that a tyrant is at liberty not to believe the best advices, he answered, "Why do you say he is at liberty not to do so, seeing he will bear the smart of it? for every man who shuts his ears to good counsel commits a fault, and this fault is always attended with some damage." And if it were said that a tyrant is permitted to put to death the men of the best parts and understanding in his State, he replied again, "Do you think he is not punished in losing his chief supports, or that he will be quit for a slight punishment? Is to govern in this manner the way to preserve himself? or rather, is it not the certain means to hasten his own ruin?"

Being asked what was the best study for man to apply himself to, he answered, "To do well;" and being asked farther whether good fortune was the effect of study, "On the contrary," said he, "I think good fortune and study to be two opposite things; for what I call good fortune is, when a man meets with what is necessary for him, without the trouble of seeking it; but when he meets with any good success after a tedious search and labour, it is an effect of study. This is what I call to do well; and I think that all who take delight in this study are for the most part successful, and gain the esteem of men, and the affection of the Deity. Such are they as have rendered themselves excellent in economy, in physic, and in politics; but he who knows not any one thing perfectly is neither useful to men, nor beloved by the gods."

CHAPTER X

SOCRATES, IN CONVERSATION WITH SEVERAL ARTIFICERS, A PAINTER, A STATUARY, AND AN ARMOURER, SHOWETH HIS SKILL AND GOOD TASTE IN THE FINER ARTS

As Socrates studied to be useful in all his conversations, so he never happened to be in company even with tradesmen but he always said something that might be of service to them. Going once into the shop of the painter Parrhasius, he entertained himself with him in the following manner: —

"Is not painting," said he, "a representation of all we see? For with a few colours you represent on a canvas mountains and caverns, light and obscurity; you cause to be observed the difference between soft things and hard, between things smooth and rough; you give youth and old age to bodies; and when you would represent a perfect beauty, it being impossible to find a body but what has some defect, your way is to regard several, and taking what is beautiful from each of them, you make one that is accomplished in all its parts."

"We do so," said Parrhasius.

"Can you represent likewise," said Socrates, "what is most charming and most lovely in the person, I mean the inclination?"

"How think you," answered Parrhasius, "we can paint what cannot be expressed by any proportion, nor with any colour, and that has nothing in common with any of those things you mentioned, and which the pencil can imitate; in a word, a thing that cannot be seen?"

"Do not the very looks of men," replied Socrates, "confess either hatred or friendship?"

"In my opinion they do," said Parrhasius. "You can then make hatred and friendship appear in the eyes?"

"I own we can."

"Do you think likewise," continued Socrates, "that they who concern themselves either in the adversity or prosperity of friends, keep the same look with those who are wholly unconcerned for either?"

"By no means," said he, "for during the prosperity of our friends, our looks are gay and full of joy, but in their adversity we look cloudy and dejected."

"This, then, may be painted likewise?"

"It may."

"Besides," said Socrates, "magnificence, generosity, meanness of mind, cowardice, modesty, prudence, insolence, rusticity, all appear in the looks of a man, whether sitting or standing."

"You say true."

"And cannot the pencil imitate all this likewise?"

"It may."

"And in which do you take most pleasure," said Socrates, "in regarding the picture of a man whose external appearance discovereth a good natural disposition, and bespeaks an honest man, or of one who wears in his face the marks of a vicious inclination?"

"There is no comparison between them," said Parrhasius.

Another time, talking with Clito the sculptor, he said to him, "I wonder not that you make so great a difference between the statue of a man who is running a race and that of one who stands his ground to wait for his antagonist with whom he is to wrestle, or to box, or to play a prize at all sorts of defence; but what ravishes the beholders is, that your statues seem to be alive. I would fain know by what art you imprint upon them this wonderful vivacity?" Clito, surprised at this question, stood considering what to answer, when Socrates went on:—"Perhaps you take great care to make them resemble the living persons, and this is the reason that they seem to live likewise."

"It is so," said Clito.

"You must then," replied Socrates, "observe very exactly in the different postures of the body what are the natural dispositions of all the parts, for when some of them stoop down, the others raise themselves up; when some are contracted, the others stretch themselves out; when some are stiff with straining, others relax themselves; and when you imitate all this, you make your statues approach very near the life."

"You say true," said Clito.

"Is it not true likewise," replied Socrates, "that it is a great satisfaction to beholders to see all the passions of a man who is in action well expressed? Thus, in the statue of a gladiator who is fighting, you must imitate the sternness of look with which he threatens his enemy; on the contrary, you must give him, when victor, a look of gaiety and content."

"There is no doubt of what you say."

"We may then conclude," said Socrates, "that it is the part of an excellent statuary to express the various affections and passions of the soul, by representing such-and-such motions and postures of the body as are commonly exerted in real life whenever the mind is so-and-so affected."

Another time, Socrates being in the shop of Pistias the armourer, who showed him some corselets that were very well made: "I admire," said Socrates to him, "the invention of these arms that cover the body in the places where it has most need of being defended, and nevertheless are no hindrance to the motions of the hands and arms; but tell me why you sell the suits of armour you make dearer than the other workmen of the city, since they are not stronger nor of better-tempered or more valuable metal?"

"I sell them dearer than others," answered Pistias, "because they are better made than theirs."

"In what does this make consist?" said Socrates, "in the weight, or in the largeness of the arms? And yet you make them not all of the same weight nor of the same size, but to fit every man."

"They must be fit," said Pistias, "otherwise they would be of no use."

"But do you not know," replied Socrates, "that some bodies are well-shaped and others not?"

"I know it well."

"How, then," continued Socrates, "can you make a well-shaped suit of armour for an ill-shaped body?"

"It will be sufficient if they are fit for him," answered Pistias; "for what is fit is well made."

"You are of opinion, then," added Socrates, "that one cannot judge whether a thing be well made, considering it merely in itself, but in regard to the person who is to use it; as if you said that a buckler is well made for him whom it fits, and in like manner of a suit of clothes and any other thing whatsoever. But I think there is another convenience in having a suit of armour well made."

"What do you take that to be?" said Pistias.

"I think," answered Socrates, "a suit of armour that is well made does not load the bearer so much as one ill made, even though it weigh as much. For ill-made arms, by pressing too much upon the shoulders, or hanging cumbrous on some other part, become almost insupportable, and greatly incommode the person that weareth them. But those arms which, as they ought, distribute an equal weight to all the parts of the body, that join upon the neck, the shuolders, the breast, the back, and the hips, may be said to be glued to the body, and to weigh nothing at all."

"For this," said Pistias, "I value the arms I make. It is true that some choose rather to part with their money for arms that are gilt and finely carved, but if with all this they fit not easy upon them, I think they buy a rich inconveniency."

Socrates went on:— "But since the body is not always in the same posture, but sometimes bends, and sometimes raises itself straight, how can arms that are very fit be convenient and easy?"

"They never can," said Pistias.

"Your opinion therefore is," said Socrates, "that the best arms are not those that are most fit, and fit closest to the body, but those that do not incommode the person that wears them."

"You, too, are of the same opinion," replied Pistias, "and you understand the matter aright."

CHAPTER XI

DISCOURSE OF SOCRATES WITH THEODOTA, AN ATHENIAN LADY, OF NO GOOD CHARACTER; WHEREIN HE ENDEAVOURETH, IN THE MOST ARTFUL AND ENGAGING MANNER, TO WIN HER OVER FROM THE CRIMINAL PLEASURES TO WHICH SHE WAS ADDICTED UNTO THE SUBLIMER AND MORE INNOCENT DELIGHTS OF PHILOSOPHY AND VIRTUE

THERE was at Athens a very beautiful lady called Theodota, who had the character of a loose dame. Some person was speaking of her in presence of Socrates, and saying that she was the most beautiful woman in the whole world; that all the painters went to see her, to draw her picture, and that they were very well received at her house. "I think," said Socrates, "we ought to go see her too, for we shall be better able to judge of her beauty after we have seen her ourselves than upon the bare relation of others." The person who began the discourse encouraged the matter, and that very moment they all went to Theodota's house. They found her with a painter who was drawing her picture; and having considered her at leisure when the painter had done, Socrates began thus: — "Do you think that we are more obliged to Theodota for having afforded us the sight of her beauty than she is to us for coming to see her? If all the advantage be on her side, it must be owned that she is obliged to us; if it be on ours, it must be confessed that we are so to her." Some of the company saying there was reason to think so, Socrates continued in these words:—"Has she not already had the advantage of receiving the praises we have given her? But it will be yet a much greater to her when we make known her merit in all the companies we come into; but as for ourselves, what do we carry from hence except a desire to enjoy the things we have seen? We go hence with souls full of love and uneasiness; and from this time forward we must obey Theodota in all she pleases to enjoin us."

"If it be so," said Theodota, "I must return you many thanks for your coming hither."

Meanwhile Socrates took notice that she was magnificently apparelled, and that her mother appeared likewise like a woman of condition. He saw a great number of women attendants elegantly dressed, and that the whole house was richly furnished. He took occasion from hence to inform himself of her circumstances in the world, and to ask her whether she had an estate in land or houses in the city, or slaves, whose labour supplied the expenses of her family.

"I have nothing," answered she, "of all this; my friends are my revenue. I subsist by their liberality."

Upon which Socrates remarked that "friendship was one of the greatest blessings in life, for that a good friend could stand one in stead of all possessions whatever." And he advised Theodota to try all her art to procure to herself some lovers and friends that might render her happy. The lady asking Socrates whether there were any artifices to be used for that purpose, he answered, "there were," and proceeded to mention several:—"Some for attracting the regard of the men, some for insinuating into their hearts; others for securing their affections and managing their passions."

Whereupon Theodota, whose soul then lay open to any impression, mistaking the virtuous design of Socrates is the whole of this discourse for an intention of another sort, cried out in raptures, "Ah! Socrates, why will not you help me to friends?"

"I will," replied Socrates, "if you can persuade me to do so."

"And what means must I use to persuade you?"

"You must invent the means," said Socrates, "if you want me to serve you."

"Then come to see me often," added Theodota.

Socrates laughed at the simplicity of the woman, and in raillery said to her, "I have not leisure enough to come and see you; I have both public and private affairs which take up too much of my time. Besides, I have mistresses who will not suffer me to be from them neither day nor night, and who against myself make use of the very charms and sorceries that I have taught them."

"And have you any knowledge in those things, too?" said she.

"Why do Apollodorus and Antisthenes," answered Socrates, "never leave me? why do Cebes and Simmias forsake Thebes for my company? This they would not do if I were not master of some charm."

"Lend it me," said Theodota, "that I may employ it against you, and charm you to come to me."

"No," said Socrates, "but I will charm you, and make you come to me."

"I will," said Theodota, "if you will promise to make me welcome."

"I promise you I will," answered Socrates, "provided there be nobody with me whom I love better than you."

CHAPTER XII

OF THE NECESSITY OF EXERCISE TO HEALTH AND STRENGTH OF BODY

AMONG others who frequented Socrates, there was a young man whose name was Epigenes, and who was very awkward in his person and behaviour, and had contracted an ill habit of body, having never learnt nor used any exercise. Socrates reproached him for it, and told him that it was unworthy of any man to be so negligent of himself. Epigenes slightly answered that he was under no obligation to do better. "You are no less obliged to it," replied Socrates, "than they who train themselves up for the Olympic Games. For do you believe that to fight for one's life against the enemies of the Republic, which we are all obliged to do when the Athenians please to command us, is a less important occasion than to contend with antagonists for a prize? How many men are there who, for want of strength, perish in fights; or have recourse to dishonourable means to seek their safety? Some are taken prisoners, and remain in slavery all the rest of their days, or are forced to pay so great a ransom, as makes them live poor and miserable ever afterwards: others are ill thought of, and their weakness is imputed to cowardice. And do you value so little all these misfortunes, which constantly attend an ill habit of body, and do they seem to you so slight? In my opinion, there are no fatigues in the exercises but what are more easy and more agreeable. But perhaps you despise the advantages of a good disposition of body:

nevertheless, they are considerable; for men in that condition enjoy a perfect health, they are robust and active, they come off from combats with honour, they escape from dangers, they succour their friends, they render great services to their country. For these reasons they are well received wherever they come, they are in good reputation with all men, they attain to the highest offices, they live the more honourably and the more at ease, and they leave their posterity the most noble examples. If, therefore, you do not practise the military exercises in public, you ought not to neglect the doing so in private, but to apply yourself to them with all possible diligence.

"To have the body active and healthy can be hurtful to you in no occasions: and since we cannot do anything without the body, it is certain that a good constitution will be of great advantage to us in all our undertakings. Even in study, where there seems to be least need of it, we know many persons who could never make any great progress for want of health. Forgetfulness, melancholy, loss of appetite, and folly, are the diseases that generally proceed from the indisposition of the body; and these diseases sometimes seize the mind with so great violence, that they wipe out even the least remembrance of what we knew before. But in health we have nothing like this to fear, and consequently there is no toil which a judicious man would not willingly undergo to avoid all these misfortunes. And, indeed, it is shameful for a man to grow old before he has tried his own strength, and seen to what degree of dexterity and perfection he can attain, which he can never know if he give himself over for useless; because dexterity and strength come not of themselves, but by practice and exercise."

CHAPTER XIII

SEVERAL APOPHTHEGMS OF SOCRATES

A certain man being vexed that he had saluted one who did not return his civility, Socrates said to him, "It is ridiculous in you to be unconcerned when you meet a sick man in the way, and to be vexed for having met a rude fellow."

2. Another was saying that he had lost his appetite and could eat nothing. Socrates, having heard it, told him he could teach him a remedy for that. The man asking what it was, "Fast," said he, "for some time, and I will warrant you will be in better health, spend less money, and eat with more satisfaction afterwards."

3. Another complained that the water which came into the cistern was warm, and nevertheless he was forced to drink it.

"You ought to be glad of it," said Socrates, "for it is a bath ready for you, whenever you have a mind to bathe yourself,"

"It is too cold to bathe in," replied the other.

"Do your servants," said Socrates, "find any inconvenience in drinking it, or in bathing in it?"

"No, but I wonder how they can suffer it."

"Is it," continued Socrates, "warmer to drink than that of the temple of Æsculapius?"

"It is not near so warm."

"You see, then," said Socrates, "that you are harder to please than your own servants, or even than the sick themselves."

4. A master having beaten his servant most cruelly, Socrates asked him why he was so angry with him. The master answered, "Because he is a drunkard, a lazy fellow who loves money, and is always idle."

"Suppose he be so," said Socrates: "but be your own judge, and tell me, which of you two deserves rather to be punished for those faults?"

5. Another made a difficulty of undertaking a journey to Olympia. "What is the reason," said Socrates to him, "that you are so much afraid of walking, you, who walk up and down about your house almost all day long? You ought to look upon this journey to be only a walk, and to think that you will walk away the morning till dinner-time, and the afternoon till supper, and thus you will insensibly find yourself at your journey's end. For it is certain that in five or six days' time you go more ground in walking up and down than you need to do in going from Athens to Olympia. I will tell you one thing more: it is much better to set out a day too soon than a day too late; for it is troublesome to be forced to go long journeys; and on the contrary, it is a great ease to have the advantage of a day beforehand. You were better therefore to hasten your departure than be obliged to make haste upon the road."

6. Another telling him that he had been a great journey, and was extremely weary, Socrates asked whether he had carried anything. The other answered that he had carried nothing but his cloak. "Were you alone?" said Socrates.

"No; I had a slave with me."

"Was not he loaded?" continued Socrates.

"Yes, for he carried all my things."

"And how did he find himself upon the road?"

"Much better than I."

"And if you had been to carry what he did, what would have become of you?"

"Alas!" said he, "I should never have been able to have done it."

"Is it not a shame," added Socrates, "in a man like you, who have gone through all the exercises, not to be able to undergo as much fatigue as his slave?"

CHAPTER XIV

SOCRATES PROPOSETH SOME REGULATIONS FOR THE BETTER MANAGEMENT OF THEIR PUBLIC FEASTS

SOCRATES having observed that in public suppers every one brought his own dish of meat, and that sometimes some brought more and others less, was wont, when this happened, to bid a servant set the least dish in the middle of the table, and to give some of it to all the company. No man could, in civility, refuse it, nor exempt himself from doing the like with his own dish, insomuch that every man had a taste of the whole, and all fared alike. This in some measure banished luxury and expensiveness from these feasts. For they who would have laid out a great deal of money in delicacies cared no longer to do so, because they would have been as much for others as for themselves.

Being one day in these assemblies, and seeing a young man who ate his meat without bread, he took occasion to rally him for it upon a question that was started touching the imposing of names. "Can we give any reason," said he, "why a man is called flesh-eater—that is to say, a devourer of flesh?—for every man eats flesh when he has it; and I do not believe it to be upon that account that a man is called so."

"Nor I neither," said one of the company.

"But," continued Socrates, "if a man takes delight to eat his meat without bread, do you not take him to be, indeed, a flesh-eater?"

"I should think it difficult to find another who better would deserve that name."

Upon which somebody else taking the word said, "What think you of him who, with a little bread only, eats a great deal of flesh?"

"I should," replied Socrates, "judge him, too, to be a flesh-eater; and whereas others ask of the gods in their prayers to give them an abundance of fruits, such men in their petitions it is likely would pray only for abundance of flesh."

The young man whom Socrates had in mind, suspecting that he spoke upon his account, took some bread, but continued still to eat a great deal of flesh with it.

Socrates perceived him, and showing him with his finger to those that sat next to him, said to them, "Take notice of your neighbour, and see whether it be the meat that makes him eat his bread, or the bread that makes him eat his meat."

In a like occasion, seeing a man sop the same morsel of meat in several sauces, he said, "Is it possible to make a sauce that will cost more, and be not so good, as one that is made by taking out of several different sauces at once? For there being more ingredients than usual, no doubt it costs more; but then because we mix things together, which the cooks never used to mingle, because they agree not well with one another, we certainly spoil the whole; and is it not a jest to be curious in having good cooks, and at the same time to be so fantastical as to alter the relish of the dishes they have dressed? Besides, when we have once got a habit of eating thus of several dishes at once, we are not so well satisfied when we have no longer that variety. Whereas a man who contents himself to eat but of one dish at a time finds no great inconvenience in having but one dish of meat for his dinner."

He made likewise this remark: that to express what the other Greeks called "to eat a meal," the Athenians said "to make good cheer;" and that the word "good" shows us that we ought to eat such things only as will neither disorder the body nor the mind, which are easily had, and purchased without great expense. From whence he inferred that they alone who live temperately and soberly can truly be said to make good cheer — that is to say, to eat well.

BOOK IV

CHAPTER I

THAT PERSONS OF GOOD NATURAL PARTS, AS WELL AS THOSE WHO HAVE PLENTIFUL FORTUNES, OUGHT NOT TO THINK THEMSELVES ABOVE INSTRUCTION. ON THE CONTRARY, THE ONE OUGHT, BY THE AID OF LEARNING, TO IMPROVE THEIR GENIUS; THE OTHER, BY THE ACQUISITION OF KNOWLEDGE, TO RENDER THEMSELVES VALUABLE

THERE was always, as we have already remarked, some improvement to be made with Socrates; and it must be owned that his company and conversation were very edifying, since even now, when he is no more among us, it is still of advantage to his friends to call him to their remembrance. And, indeed, whether he spoke to divert himself, or whether he spoke seriously, he always let slip some remarkable instructions for the benefit of all that heard him.

He used often to say he was in love, but it was easy to see it was not with the beauty of one's person that he was taken, but with the virtues of his mind.

The marks of a good genius, he said, were these—a good judgment, a retentive memory, and an ardent desire of useful knowledge; that is to say, when a person readily learns what he is taught, and strongly retains what he has learnt, as also when he is curious to know all that is necessary to the good government either of a family or of a republic; in a word, when one desires to obtain a thorough knowledge of mankind and of whatever relates to human affairs. And his opinion was that when these good natural parts are cultivated as they ought, such men are not only happy themselves, and govern their families prudently, but are capable likewise to render others happy, and to make republics flourish.

On the one hand, therefore, whenever he met with any who believed themselves men of parts, and for that reason neglected to be instructed, he proved to them that men of the best natural parts are they who have most need of instruction; and to this purpose he alleged the example of a high-mettled horse, who, having more courage and more strength than others, does us very great service, if he be broke and managed in his youth; but if that be neglected, he grows so vicious and unruly that we know not what to do with him. Thus also dogs of a good breed, and that by nature are the most strong and mettlesome, are excellent for game, if they are well taught; otherwise they are apt to become high rangers and at no command. In like manner among men they who are blessed with the greatest advantages of Nature, to whom she has given the most courage and the greatest strength to enable them to succeed in their undertakings, are likewise the most virtuous, and do more good than others, when they meet with a good education; but if they remain without instruction they fall into an excess of ill, and become most pernicious to themselves and others. Merely for want of knowing their duty they often engage themselves in very wicked designs; and being imperious and violent, it is very difficult to keep them within bounds and to make them change their resolution, which is the reason they do a great deal of mischief.

On the other hand, when he saw any of those men who pique themselves on their estates, and who believe because they are men of high condition that they are above instruction, or have no need of it, because their riches alone are sufficient to gain them the esteem of the world, and to make them succeed in all their undertakings, he endeavoured to convince them of their error, and to show them that they, too, have need of instruction. He told them that that man is a fool who imagines with himself that he can know the things that are useful from those that are hurtful, without having ever learnt the difference; or who, not discerning between them, fondly thinks that because he has wherewithal to buy whatever he has a mind to, he can therefore do whatever may tend to his advantage; or who, judging himself incapable to do what is useful for himself, thinks, nevertheless, that he is well in the world, and in a safe and happy condition of life. That it is likewise a folly for a man to persuade himself that, being rich and having no merit, he will pass for a man of parts; or that, not having the reputation of being a man of parts, he shall nevertheless be esteemed.

CHAPTER II

CONFERENCE BETWEEN SOCRATES AND EUTHYDEMUS, IN WHICH HE CONVINCES THAT YOUNG MAN, WHO HAD A GREAT OPINION OF HIMSELF, THAT HE KNEW NOTHING

WHEN Socrates, on the other hand, found any who soothe themselves up in the belief that they are well instructed, and who boast of their own sufficiency, he never failed to chastise the vanity of such persons. Of his conduct in this particular I will relate the following instance:—

He had been told that Euthydemus had bought up several works of the most celebrated poets and sophists, and that this acquisition had so puffed him up with arrogance, that he already esteemed himself the greatest man for learning and parts of any of the age, and pretended to no less than being the first man of the city, either for negotiating or for discoursing in public. Nevertheless, he was still so young that he was not admitted into the assemblies of the people, and if he had any affair to solicit he generally came and placed himself in one of the shops that were near the courts of justice. Socrates, having observed his station, failed not to go thither likewise with two or three of his friends; and there, being fallen into discourse, this question was started: Whether it was by the improving conversation of philosophers or by the strength of his natural parts only, that Themistocles surpassed all his countrymen in wisdom and valour, and advanced himself to such a high rank and to so great esteem, that all the Republic cast their eyes upon him whenever their affairs required the conduct of a man of bravery and wisdom? Socrates, who had a mind to reflect upon Euthydemus, answered that "a man must be very stupid to believe that mechanic arts (which are comparatively things but of small importance) cannot be learnt without masters; and yet that the art of governing of States, which is a thing of the greatest moment and that requires the greatest effort of human prudence, comes of itself into the mind." And this was all that passed in this first interview.

After this Socrates, observing that Euthydemus always avoided being in his company, lest he should be taken for one of his admirers, attacked him more openly; and once when he happened to be where he was, addressed himself to the rest of the company in these words: — "Certainly, gentlemen, by what may be conjectured from the studies of this young man, it is very likely that when he shall have attained the age that permits him to be present in the assemblies of the people, if any important affair come to be debated there, he will not fail to give his judgment of it; and in my opinion he would introduce his harangue by a very pleasant exordium, if he should begin with giving them to understand that he had never learnt anything of any man whatsoever; he must address himself to them in words to this purpose: —

"'Gentlemen, I have never been taught anything, I never frequented the conversation of men of parts, I never gave myself the trouble to look out for a master that was able to instruct me. On the contrary, gentlemen, I have not only had an aversion to learn from others, but I should even have been very sorry to have it believed I had done so; nevertheless, I will venture to tell you what chance shall suggest to me in this present occasion.' At this rate they who present themselves to be received physicians might introduce a like discourse as thus: — 'Gentlemen, I have never had any master to teach me this science; for, indeed, I would never learn it, nor even have the repute of having learnt it; nevertheless, admit me a physician, and I will endeavour to become learned in the art by making experiments on your own bodies.'"

All the company fell a-laughing at this pleasant preface, and from that time Euthydemus never avoided Socrates' company as he had done before; but he never offered to speak, believing that his silence would be an argument of his modesty. Socrates, being desirous to rally him out of that mistaken notion, spoke to him in this manner:—

"I wonder that they who desire to learn to play upon the lute, or to ride well, do not endeavour to learn it alone by themselves; but that they look out for masters, resolved to do everything they bid them, and to believe all they say, there being no other way to arrive at perfection in those arts; and that they who hope one day to govern the Republic, and to declaim before the people, imagine they can become fit to do so of themselves all of a sudden. Nevertheless, it must be owned that these employments are more difficult than the others, since among the great number of persons who push themselves into office so few discharge their duty as they ought. This shows us that more labour and diligence is required in such as would capacitate themselves for those offices than for anything else."

By these discourses, Socrates having prepared the mind of Euthydemus to hearken to what he intended to say to him, and to enter into conference with him, he came another time by himself into the same shop, and taking a seat next to this young man—"I have heard," said he to him, "that you have been curious in buying a great many good books."

"I have," said Euthydemus, "and continue to do so every day, designing to have as many as I can get."

"I commend you very much," said Socrates, "for choosing rather to hoard up a treasure of learning and knowledge than of money. For you testify by so doing that you are not of opinion that riches, or silver and gold, can render one more valuable, that is to say, a wiser or a better man; but that it is only the writings and precepts of the philosophers and other fine writers that are the true riches, because they enrich with virtue the minds of those that possess them." Euthydemus was pleased to hear him say this, believing that he approved his method; and Socrates, perceiving his satisfaction, went on: "But what is your design of making a collection of so many books? Do you intend to be a physician? There are many books in that science."

"That is not my design," said Euthydemus.

"Will you be an architect, then?" said Socrates, "for that art requires a learned man. Or do you study geometry or astrology?"

"None of them."

"Do you mean to be a reciter of heroic verses?" continued Socrates, "for I have been told that you have all Homer's works."

"Not in the least," answered Euthydemus, "for I have observed that men of that profession know indeed a great many verses by heart, but for anything else they are for the most part very impertinent."

"Perhaps you are in love with that noble science that makes politicians and economists, and that renders men capable to govern, and to be useful to others and to themselves?"

"That is what I endeavour to learn," said Euthydemus, "and what I passionately desire to know."

"It is a sublime science," replied Socrates; "it is that we call the royal science, because it truly is the science of kings. But have you weighed this point, whether a man can excel in that science without being an honest man?"

"I have," said the young man, "and am even of opinion that none but honest men can be good citizens."

"And are you an honest man?" said Socrates.

"I hope I am," answered Euthydemus, "as honest a man as another."

"Tell me," said Socrates, "can we know who are honest men by what they do, as we know what trade a man is of by his work?"

"We may."

"Then," said Socrates, "as architects show us their works, can honest men show us theirs likewise?"

"No doubt of it," replied Euthydemus; "and it is no difficult task to show you which are the works of justice, and which those of injustice, that we so often hear mentioned."

"Shall we," said Socrates, "make two characters, the one (J) to signify justice, the other (I) to denote injustice; and write under one of them all the works that belong to justice, and under the other all that belong to injustice?"

"Do," said Euthydemus, "if you think fit."

Socrates, having done what he proposed, continued thus his discourse: — "Do not men tell lies?"

"Very often," answered Euthydemus.

"Under which head shall we put lying?"

"Under that of injustice," said Euthydemus.

"Do not men sometimes cheat?"

"Most certainly."

"Where shall we put cheating?" said Socrates.

"Under injustice."

"And doing wrong to one's neighbour?"

"There too."

"And selling of free persons into slavery?"

"Still in the same place."

"And shall we write none of all these," said Socrates, "under the head of justice?"

"Not one of them," answered Euthydemus; "it would be strange if we did."

"But what," replied Socrates, "when a general plunders an enemy's city, and makes slaves of all the inhabitants, shall we say that he commits an injustice?"

"By no means."

"Shall we own, then, that he does an act of justice?"

"Without doubt."

"And when he circumvents his enemies in the war, does he not do well?"

"Very well."

"And when he ravages their land, and takes away their cattle and their corn, does he not do justly?"

"It is certain he does," said Euthydemus; "and when I answered you that all these actions were unjust, I thought you had spoken of them in regard only of friend to friend."

"We must, therefore," replied Socrates, "put among the actions of justice those very actions we have ascribed to injustice, and we will only establish this distinction, that it is just to behave ourselves so towards our enemies; but that to treat our friends thus is an injustice, because we ought to live with them uprightly, and without any deceit."

"I think so," said Euthydemus.

"But," continued Socrates, "when a general sees that his troops begin to be disheartened, if he make them believe that a great reinforcement is coming to him, and by that stratagem inspires fresh courage into the soldiers, under what head shall we put this lie?"

"Under the head of justice," answered Euthydemus.

"And when a child will not take the physic that he has great need of, and his father makes it be given him in a mess of broth, and by that means the child recovers his health, to which shall we ascribe this deceit?"

"To justice likewise."

"And if a man, who sees his friend in despair, and fears he will kill himself, hides his sword from him, or takes it out of his hands by force, what shall we say of this violence?"

"That it is just," replied Euthydemus.

"Observe what you say," continued Socrates; "for it follows from your answers that we are not always obliged to live with our friends uprightly, and without any deceit, as we agreed we were."

"No; certainly we are not, and if I may be permitted to retract what I said, I change my opinion very freely."

"It is better," said Socrates, "to change an opinion than to persist in a wrong one. But there is still one point which we must not pass over without inquiry, and this relates to those whose deceits are prejudicial to their friends; for I ask you, which are most unjust, they who with premeditate design cheat their friends, or they who do it through inadvertency?"

"Indeed," said Euthydemus, "I know not what to answer, nor what to believe, for you have so fully refuted what I have said, that what appeared to me before in one light appears to me now in another. Nevertheless, I will venture to say that he is the most unjust who deceives his friend deliberately."

"Do you think," said Socrates, "that one may learn to be just and honest, as well as we learn to read and write?"

"I think we may."

"Which," added Socrates, "do you take to be the most ignorant, he who reads wrong on purpose, or he who reads wrong because he can read no better?"

"The last of them," answered Euthydemus; "for the other who mistakes for pleasure need not mistake when he pleases."

"Then," inferred Socrates, "he who reads wrong deliberately knows how to read; but he who reads wrong without design is an ignorant man."

"You say true."

"Tell me likewise," pursued Socrates, "which knows best what ought to be done, and what belongs to justice, he who lies and cheats with premeditate design, or he who deceives without intention to deceive?"

"It is most plain," said Euthydemus, "that it is he who deceives with premeditate design."

"But you said," replied Socrates, "that he who can read is more learned than he who cannot read?"

"I did so."

"Therefore he who best knows which are the duties of justice is more just than he that knows them not."

"It seems to be so," answered Euthydemus, "and I know not well how I came to say what I did."

"Indeed," said Socrates, "you often change your opinion, and contradict what you say; and what would you yourself think of any man who pretended to tell the truth, and yet never said the same thing; who, in pointing out to you the same road, should show you sometimes east, sometimes west, and who, in telling the same sum, should find more money at one time than another; what would you think of such a man?"

"He would make all men think," answered Euthydemus, "that he knew nothing of what he pretended to know."

Socrates urged him yet further, and asked him: "Have you ever heard say that some men have abject and servile minds?"

"I have."

"Is it said of them because they are learned or because they are ignorant?"

"Surely because they are ignorant."

"Perhaps," said Socrates, "it is because they understand not the trade of a smith?"

"Not in the least for that."

"Is it because they know not how to build a house, or to make shoes?"

"By no means," said Euthydemus; "for most who are skilled in such professions have likewise abject and servile minds,"

"This character, then," pursued Socrates, "must be given to those who are ignorant of the noble sciences, and who know not what is just nor what is honourable?"

"I believe so."

"We ought, therefore, Euthydemus, to do all we can to avoid falling into that ignominious ignorance that sinks us down so low."

"Alas, Socrates!" cried he out, "I will not lie for the matter; I thought I knew something in philosophy, and that I had learnt whatever was requisite to be known by a man who desired to make a practice of virtue; but judge how much I am afflicted to see that, after all my labours, I am not able to answer you concerning things which I ought chiefly to know; and yet I am at a loss what method to pursue in order to render myself more capable and knowing in the things I desire to understand." Upon this, Socrates asked him whether he had ever been at Delphi, and Euthydemus answered that he had been there twice.

"Did you not take notice," said Socrates, "that somewhere on the front of the temple there is this inscription, 'KNOW THYSELF'?"

"I remember," answered he, "I have read it there."

"It is not enough," replied Socrates, "to have read it. Have you been the better for this admonition? Have you given yourself the trouble to consider what you are?"

"I think I know that well enough," replied the young man, "for I should have found it very difficult to have known any other thing if I had not known myself."

"But for a man to know himself well," said Socrates, "it is not enough that he knows his own name; for, as a man that buys a horse cannot be certain that he knows what he is before he has ridden him, to see whether he be quiet or restive, whether he be mettlesome or dull, whether he be fleet or heavy—in short, before he has made trial of all that is good and bad in him—in like manner, a man cannot say that he knows himself before he has tried what he is fit for, and what he is able to do."

"It is true," said Euthydemus, "that whoever knows not his own strength knows not himself."

"But," continued Socrates, "who sees not of how great advantage this knowledge is to man, and how dangerous it is to be mistaken in this affair? for he who knows himself knows likewise what is good for himself. He sees what he is able to do, and what he is not able to do; by applying himself to things that he can do, he gets his bread with pleasure, and is happy; and by not attempting to do the things he cannot do, he avoids the danger of falling into errors, and of seeing himself miserable. By knowing himself, he knows likewise how to judge of others, and to make use of their services for his own advantage, either to procure himself some good, or to protect himself from some misfortune; but he who knows not himself, and is mistaken in the opinion he has of his own abilities, mistakes likewise in the knowledge of others, and in the conduct of his own affairs. He is ignorant of what is necessary for him, he knows not what he undertakes, nor comprehends the means he makes use of, and this is the reason that success never attends his enterprises, and that he always falls into misfortunes. But the man who sees clear into his own designs generally obtains the end he proposes to himself, and at the same time gains reputation and honour. For this reason, even his equals are well pleased to follow his advices; and they whose affairs are in disorder implore his assistance, and throw themselves into his hands, depending upon his prudence to retrieve their affairs, and to restore them to their former good condition. But he who undertakes he knows not what, generally makes an ill choice, and succeeds yet worse; and the present damage is not the only punishment he undergoes for his temerity. He is disgraced for ever; all men laugh at him, all men despise and speak ill of him. Consider likewise what happens to Republics who mistake their own strength, and declare war against States more powerful than themselves; some are utterly ruined, others lose their liberty, and are compelled to receive laws from the conquerors."

"I am fully satisfied," said Euthydemus, "that a great deal depends on the knowledge of oneself. I hope you will now tell me by what a man must begin to examine himself."

"You know," said Socrates, "what things are good and what are bad?"

"Indeed," answered Euthydemus, "if I knew not that, I were the most ignorant of all men."

"Then tell me your thoughts of this matter," said Socrates.

"First," said Euthydemus, "I hold that health is a good and sickness an evil, and that whatever contributes to either of them partakes of the same qualities. Thus nourishment and the exercises that keep the body in health are very good; and, on the contrary, those that cause diseases are hurtful."

"But would it not be better to say," replied Socrates, "that health and sickness are both good when they are the causes of any good, and that they are both bad when they are the causes of any ill?"

"And when can it ever happen," said Euthydemus, "that health is the cause of any ill, and sickness the cause of any good?"

"This may happen," answered Socrates, "when troops are raised for any enterprise that proves fatal; when men are embarked who are destined to perish at sea; for men who are in health may be involved in these misfortunes, when they who, by reason of their infirmities, are left at home, will be exempted from the mischiefs in which the others perish."

"You say true," said Euthydemus, "but you see, too, that men who are in health are present in fortunate occasions, while they who are confined to their beds cannot be there."

"It must therefore be granted," said Socrates, "that these things which are sometimes useful and sometimes hurtful are not rather good than bad."

"That is, indeed, the consequence of your argument," replied Euthydemus; "but it cannot be denied that knowledge is a good thing; for what is there in which a knowing man has not the advantage of an ignorant one?"

"And have you not read," said Socrates, "what happened to Dædalus for his knowing so many excellent arts, and how, being fallen into the hands of Minos, he was detained by force, and saw himself at once banished from his country and stripped of his liberty? To complete his misfortune, flying away with his son, he was the occasion of his being miserably lost, and could not, after all, escape in his own person; for, falling into the hands of barbarians, he was again made a slave. Know you not likewise the adventure of Palamedes, who was so envied by Ulysses for his great capacity, and who perished wretchedly by the calumnious artifices of that rival? How many great men likewise has the King of Persia caused to be seized and carried away because of their admirable parts, and who are now languishing under him in a perpetual slavery?"

"But, granting this to be as you say," added Euthydemus, "you will certainly allow good fortune to be a good?"

"I will," said Socrates, "provided this good fortune consists in things that are undoubtedly good."

"And how can it be that the things which. compose good fortune should not be infallibly good?"

"They are," answered Socrates, "unless you reckon among them beauty and strength of body, riches, honours, and other things of that nature."

"And how can a man be happy without them?"

"Rather," said Socrates, "how can a man be happy with things that are the causes of so many misfortunes? For many are daily corrupted because of their beauty; many who presume too much on their own strength are oppressed under the burden of their undertakings. Among the rich, some are lost in luxury, and others fall into the snares of those that wait for their estates. And lastly, the reputation and honours that are acquired in Republics are often the cause of their ruin who possess them."

"Certainly," said Euthydemus, "if I am in the wrong to praise good fortune, I know not what we ought to ask of the Deity."

"Perhaps, too," replied Socrates, "you have never considered it, because you think you know it well enough.

"But," continued he, changing the subject of their discourse, "seeing you are preparing yourself to enter upon the government of our Republic, where the people are master, without doubt you have reflected on the nature of this State, and know what a democracy is?"

"You ought to believe I do."

"And do you think it possible," said Socrates, "to know what a democracy or popular State is without knowing what the people is?"

"I do not think I can."

"And what is the people?" said Socrates.

"Under that name," answered Euthydemus, 'I mean the poor citizens."

"You know, then, who are the poor?"

"I do," said Euthydemus.

"Do you know, too, who are the rich?"

"I know that too."

"Tell me, then, who are the rich and who are the poor?"

"I take the poor," answered Euthydemus, "to be those who have not enough to supply their necessary expenses, and the rich to be they who have more than they have occasion for."

"But have you observed," replied Socrates, "that there are certain persons who, though they have very little, have nevertheless enough, and even lay up some small matter out of it; and, on the contrary, there are others who never have enough how great soever their estates and possessions are?"

"You put me in mind," said Euthydemus, "of something very much to the purpose, for I have seen even some princes so necessitous that they have been compelled to take away their subjects' estates, and to commit many injustices."

"We must, then," said Socrates, "place such princes in the rank of the poor, and those who have but small estates, yet manage them well, in the number of the rich."

"I must give consent to all you say," answered Euthydemus, "for I am too ignorant to contradict you; and I think it will be best for me, from henceforward, to hold my peace, for I am almost ready to confess that I know nothing at all."

Having said this, he withdrew, full of confusion and self-contempt beginning to be conscious to himself that he was indeed a person of little or no account at all. Nor was he the only person whom Socrates had thus convinced of their ignorance and insufficiency, several of whom never came more to see him, and valued him the less for it. But Euthydemus did not act like them. On the contrary, he believed it impossible for him to improve his parts but by frequently conversing with Socrates, insomuch that he never left him, unless some business of moment called him away, and he even took delight to imitate some of his actions. Socrates, seeing him thus altered from what he was, was tender of saying anything to him that might irritate or discourage him; but took care to speak more freely and plainly to him of the things he ought to know and apply himself to.

CHAPTER III

PROOFS OF A KIND SUPERINTENDING PROVIDENCE. — WHAT RETURNS OF GRATITUDE AND DUTY MEN OUGHT TO MAKE TO GOD FOR HIS FAVOURS. — AN HONEST AND GOOD LIFE THE BEST SONG OF THANKSGIVING OR THE MOST ACCEPTABLE SACRIFICE TO THE DEITY

As Socrates considered, virtue and piety as the two grand pillars of a State, and was fully persuaded that all other qualifications whatever, without the knowledge and practice of these, would, instead of enabling men to do good, serve, on the contrary, to render them more wicked and more capable of doing mischief. For that reason he never pressed his friends to enter into any public office until he had first instructed them in their duty to God and mankind. But, above all, he endeavoured to instil into their minds pious sentiments of the Deity, frequently displaying before them high and noble descriptions of the Divine power, wisdom, and goodness. But seeing several have already written what they had heard him say in divers occasions upon this subject, I will content myself with relating some things which he said to Euthydemus when I myself was present.

"Have you never reflected, Euthydemus, on the great goodness of the Deity in giving to men whatever they want?"

"Indeed, I never have," answered he.

"You see," replied Socrates, "how very necessary light is for us, and how the gods give it us."

"You say true," answered Euthydemus, "and without light we should be like the blind."

"But because we have need of repose they have given us the night to rest in; the night, which, of all times, is the fittest for repose."

"You are in the right," said Euthydemus, "and we ought to render them many praises for it."

"Moreover," continued Socrates, "as the sun is a luminous body, and by the brightness of his beams discovers to us all visible things, and shows us the hours of the day; and as, on the contrary, the night is dusky and obscure, they have made the stars to appear, which, during the absence of the day, mark the hours to us, by which means we can do many things we have occasion for. They have likewise made the moon to shine, which not only shows us the hours of the night, but teaches us to know the time of the month."

"All this is true," said Euthydemus.

"Have you not taken notice likewise that having need of nourishment, they supply us with it by the means of the earth? How excellently the seasons are ordered for the fruits of the earth, of which we have such an abundance, and so great a variety, that we find, not only wherewith to supply our real wants but to satisfy even luxury itself."

"This goodness of the gods," cried Euthydemus, "is an evidence of the great love they bear to men."

"What say you," continued Socrates, "to their having given us water, which is so necessary for all things? For it is that which assists the earth to produce the fruits, and that contributes, with the influences from above, to bring them to maturity; it helps to nourish us, and by being mingled with what we eat, makes it more easily got ready, more useful, and more delightful; in short, being of so universal an use, is it not an admirable providence that has made it so common? What say you to their having given us fire, which defends us from cold, which lights us when it is dark, which is necessary to us in all trades, and which we cannot be without in the most excellent and useful inventions of men?"

"Without exaggeration," said Euthydemus, "this goodness is immense."

"What say you, besides," pursued Socrates, "to see that after the winter the sun comes back to us, and that proportionably as he brings the new fruits to maturity, he withers and dries those whose season is going over; that after having done us this service he retires that his heat may not incommode us; and then, when he is gone back to a certain point, which he cannot transgress, without putting us in danger of dying with cold, he returns again to retake his place in this part of the heavens, where his presence is most advantageous to us? And because we should not be able to support either cold or heat, if we passed in an instant from one extreme to the other, do you not admire that this planet approaches us and withdraws himself from us by so just and slow degrees, that we arrive at the two extremes without almost perceiving the change?"

"All these things," said Euthydemus, "make me doubt whether the gods have anything to do but to serve mankind. One thing puts me to a stand, that the irrational animals participate of all these advantages with us."

"How!" said Socrates, "and do you then doubt whether the animals themselves are in the world for any other end than for the service of man? What other animals do, like us, make use of horses, of oxen, of dogs, of goats, and of the rest? Nay, I am of opinion, that man receives not so much advantage from the earth as from the animals; for the greatest part of mankind live not on the fruits of the earth, but nourish themselves with milk, cheese, and the flesh of beasts; they get the mastery over them, they make them tame, and use them to their great advantage in war and for the other necessities of life."

"I own it," said Euthydemus, "for some of them are much stronger than man, and yet are so obedient to him, that he does with them whatever he pleases."

"Admire yet further the goodness of the gods," said Socrates, "and consider, that as there is in the world an infinite number of excellent and useful things, but of very different natures, they have given us external senses, which correspond to each of those sensible objects, and by means of which senses we can perceive and enjoy all of them. They have, besides, endued us with reason and understanding, which enableth us to discern between those things that the senses discover to us, to inquire into the different natures of things useful and things hurtful, and so to know by experience which to choose and which to reject. They have likewise given us speech, by means whereof we communicate our thoughts to each other, and instruct one another in the knowledge of whatever is excellent and good; by which also we publish our laws and govern States. In fine, as we cannot always foresee what is to happen to us, nor know what it will be best for us to do, the gods offer us likewise their assistance by the means of the oracles; they discover the future to us when we go to consult them, and teach us how to behave ourselves in the affairs of life."

Here Euthydemus, interrupting him, said, "And indeed these gods are in this respect more favourable to you than to the rest of mankind, since, without expecting you to consult them, they give you notice of what you ought or ought not to do."

"You will allow, therefore, that I told you true," said Socrates, "when I told you there were gods, and that they take great care of men; but expect not that they will appear to you, and present themselves before your eyes. Let it suffice you to behold their works, and to adore them, and be persuaded that this is the way by which they manifest themselves to men, for among all the gods that are so liberal to us there is not one who renders himself visible to confer on us his favours. And that Supreme God, who built the universe, and who supports this great work, whose every part is accomplished in beauty and goodness; He, who is the cause that none of its parts grow old with time, and that they preserve themselves always in an immortal vigour, who is the cause, besides, that they inviolably obey His laws with a readiness that surpasses our imagination; He, I say, is visible enough in the so many wondrous works of which He is author, but our eyes cannot penetrate even into His throne to behold Him in these great occupations, and in that manner it is that He is always invisible. Do but consider that the sun, who seems to be exposed to the sight of all the world, does not suffer us to gaze fixedly upon him, and whoever has the temerity to undertake it is punished with sudden blindness. Besides, whatever the gods make use of is invisible; the thunder is lanced from above, it shatters all it finds in its way, but we see it not fall, we see it not strike, we see it not return. The winds are invisible, though we see the desolations they daily make, and easily feel when they grow boisterous. If there be anything in man that partakes of the divine nature it is his soul, which, beyond all dispute, guides and governs him, and yet we cannot see it. Let all this, therefore, teach you not to neglect or disbelieve the Deity, because He is invisible; learn to know His presence and power from the visible effects of it in the world around you; be persuaded of the universal care and providence of the all-surrounding Deity from the blessings He showers down upon all His creatures, and be sure to worship and serve this God in a becoming manner."

"I am sure," said Euthydemus, "I shall never derogate from the respect due to the gods; and I am even troubled that every man cannot sufficiently acknowledge the benefits he receives from them."

"Be not afflicted at that," said Socrates, "for you know what answer the Delphian Oracle is wont to return to those who inquire what they ought to do in order to make an acceptable sacrifice. 'Follow the custom of your country,' says he to them. Now, it is a custom received in all places for every man to sacrifice to them according to his power; and by consequence there is no better nor more pious a way of honouring the gods than that, since they themselves ordain and approve it. It is indeed a truth that we ought not to spare anything of what we are able to offer, for that would be a manifest contempt. When, therefore, a man has done all that is in his power to do, he ought to fear nothing and hope all; for, from whence can we reasonably hope for more, than from those in whose power it is to do us the greatest good? And by what other way can we more easily obtain it, than by making ourselves acceptable to them? And how can we better make ourselves acceptable to them, than by doing their will?"

This is what Socrates taught, and by this doctrine, which was always accompanied with an exemplary devotion, he greatly advanced his friends in piety.

CHAPTER IV

INSTANCES OF THE INVIOLABLE INTEGRITY OF SOCRATES. — HIS CONVERSATION WITH HIPPIAS CONCERNING JUSTICE

CONCERNING justice, it cannot be said that Socrates concealed his opinion of it, for he plainly revealed his sentiments by his actions, as well in public as in private, making it his business to serve every man, and to obey the magistrates and the laws; insomuch, that as well in the army as in the city, his obedience and uprightness rendered him remarkable above all others. He fully discovered the integrity of his soul, when he presided in the assemblies of the people; he would never pass a decree that was contrary to the laws; he alone defended the cause of justice against the efforts of the multitude, and opposed a violence which no man but himself was able to resist. Again, when the Thirty commanded him anything that was unjust, he did not obey them. Thus, when they forbid him to speak to the young men, he regarded not their inhibition; and when they gave orders to him, as well as to some other citizens, to bring before them a certain man, whom they intended to put to death, he alone would do nothing in it, because that order was unjust. In like manner when he was accused by Melitas, though in such occasions others endeavour to gain their judges by flatteries and ignominious solicitations, which often procure them their pardon, he would not put in practice any of these mean artifices that are repugnant to the laws, and yet he might very easily have got himself acquitted, if he could have prevailed with himself to comply in the least with the custom; but he chose rather to die in an exact observance of the laws, than to save his life by acting contrary to them, for he utterly abhorred all mean or indirect practices; and this was the answer he gave to several of his friends who advised him to the contrary.

Since I am now illustrating the character of Socrates with regard to justice, I will, at the same time, relate a conversation I remember he had with Hippias of Elis on that subject.

It was a long while that Hippias had not been at Athens; and being arrived there, he happened to come to a place where Socrates was discoursing with some persons, and telling them that if any one had a mind to learn a trade, there wanted not masters to teach him; nay, that if one would have a horse trained up there were persons enough to undertake it; but that if one desired to learn to be a good man, or to have his son, or any of his family taught to be so, it would be difficult to know to whom to apply himself. Hippias rallying him, said:— "What! Socrates, you are still repeating the same things I heard you say so long ago."

"Nay, more," replied Socrates, "and always upon the same subject; but you, perhaps, being learned as you are, do not always say the same thing upon the same subject."

"Indeed," said Hippias, "I always endeavour to say something new."

"Is it possible," replied Socrates? "Pray tell me if you were asked how many letters there are in my name, and which they are, would you answer sometimes in one manner and sometimes in another? Or if you were asked whether twice five be not ten, would you not always say the same thing?"

"In subjects like those," said Hippias, "I should be obliged to say the same thing as well as you; but since we are upon the theme of justice, I believe I can now say some things of it, against which, neither you nor any man else can make any objection."

"Good God!" cried Socrates, "what a mighty boast is here! Upon my word, Hippias, you have made an admirable discovery! and you have reason to value yourself upon it; for, let me tell you, if you can establish one single opinion of justice, the judges will be no longer divided in their sentiments, there will be no more quarrels, no more suits at law, no more seditions among citizens, no more wars between republics. Indeed, it much troubles me to leave you before you have taught me this secret, which you say you have discovered."

"I give you my word," answered Hippias, "that I will tell you nothing of it, till you have first declared your own opinion concerning justice; for it is your old way to interrogate others, and then to laugh at them by refuting what they have said; but you never make known your own opinions, that you may not be obliged to give a reason for them."

"Why do you lay this to my charge," said Socrates, "since I am continually showing to all the world what are the things I believe to be just?"

"How do you show it?" said Hippias.

"If I explain it not by my words," answered Socrates, "my actions speak it sufficiently; and do you think that actions deserve not rather to be believed than words?"

"Much rather," said Hippias, "because many may say one thing, and do another; nay, we see that, in fact, many who preach up justice to others are very unjust themselves; but this cannot be said of a man whose every action is good, and that never in his life did an unjust thing."

"Have you known, then," said Socrates, "that I have accused any man out of malice, that I have sown dissension among friends, that I have raised seditions in the Republic; in short, that I have committed any other sort of injustice?"

"Not in the least," said he.

"Well, then," added Socrates, " do you not take him to be just who commits no manner of injustice?"

"It is plain, now," said Hippias, "that you intend to get loose, and that you will not speak your mind freely, nor give us an exact definition of justice. For all this while you have only shown what just men do not, but not what they do."

"I should have thought," said Socrates, "I had given at once a good definition, and a clear instance of justice, when I called it an aversion from doing injustice. But since you will not allow it to be so, see whether this will satisfy you: I say, then, that justice 'is nothing but the observance of the laws.'"

"You mean," said Hippias, "that to observe the laws is to be just?"

"Yes," answered Socrates.

"I cannot comprehend your thought," said Hippias.

"Do you not know," pursued Socrates, "what the laws in a State are?"

"The laws," answered Hippias, "are what the citizens have ordained by an universal consent."

"Then," inferred Socrates, "he who lives conformably to those ordinances observes the laws; and he who acts contrary to them is a transgressor of the laws."

"You say true."

"Is it not likewise true," continued Socrates, "that he who obeys these ordinances does justly, and that he obeys them not does unjustly?"

"Yes."

"But," said Socrates, "he who acts justly is just, and he who acts unjustly is unjust?"

"Without doubt."

"Therefore," said Socrates, "whosoever observes the laws is just, and whosoever observes them not is unjust."

"But how can it be imagined," objected Hippias, "that the laws are a good thing, and that it is good to obey them, since even they that made them mend, alter, and repeal them so often?"

To this Socrates answered, "When you blame those who obey the laws, because they are subject to be abrogated, you do the same thing as if you laughed at your enemies for keeping themselves in a good posture of defence during the war, because you might tell them that the peace will one day be made: and thus you would condemn those who generously expose their lives for the service of their country. Do you know," added he, "that Lycurgus could never have rendered the Republic of Sparta more excellent than other States if he had not made it his chief care to incline the citizens most exactly to observe the laws? This, too, is what all good magistrates aim at, because a Republic that is obedient to the laws is happy in peace, and invincible in war. Moreover, you know that concord is a great happiness in a State. It is daily recommended to the people; and it is an established custom all over Greece to make the citizens swear to live in good understanding with one another, and each of them takes an oath to do so. Now, I do not believe that this unity is exacted of them, only that they might choose the same company of comedians, or of musicians, nor that they might give their approbation to the same poets, or all take delight in the same diversions, but that they may all unanimously obey the laws, because that obedience is the security and the happiness of the State. Concord, therefore, is so necessary, that without it good polity and authority cannot subsist in any State, nor good economy and order in any family.

"In our private capacity, likewise, how advantageous is it to obey the laws? By what means can we more certainly avoid punishments, and deserve rewards? What more prudent conduct can we observe, always to gain our suits at law, and never to be cast! To whom should we with greater confidence trust our estates or our children, than to him who makes a conscience of observing the laws? Who can deserve more of his country? whom can she more safely entrust with public posts, and on whom can she more justly bestow the highest honours, than on the good and honest man? Who will discharge himself better of his duty towards his father or his mother, towards his relations or his domestics, towards his friends, his fellow-citizens, or his guests? To whom will the enemy rather trust for the observing of a truce, or for the performance of a treaty of peace? With whom would we rather choose to make an alliance? To whom will the allies more readily give the command of their armies, or the government of their towns? From whom can we rather hope for a grateful return of a kindness than from a man who strictly obeys the laws? and, by consequence, to whom will men be more ready to do good turns, than to him of whose gratitude they are certain? With whom will men be better pleased to contract a friendship, and, consequently, against whom will men be less inclined to commit acts of hostility, than against that person who has everybody for his well-wisher and friend, and few or none for his ill-wishers or enemies? These, Hippias, are the advantages of observing the laws. And now, having shown you that the observance of the laws is the same thing with justice, if you are of another opinion, pray let me know it."

"Indeed, Socrates," answered Hippias, "what you have said of justice agrees exactly with my sentiments of it."

"Have you never heard," continued Socrates, "of certain laws that are not written?"

"You mean the laws," answered Hippias, "which are received all over the earth."

"Do you think, then," added Socrates, "that it was all mankind that made them?"

"That is impossible," said Hippias, "because all men cannot be assembled in the same place, and they speak not all of them the same language."

"Who, then, do you think gave us these laws?"

"The gods," answered Hippias; "for the first command to all men is to adore the gods."

"And is it not likewise commanded everywhere to honour one's father and mother?"

"Yes, certainly," said Hippias.

Socrates went on: — "And that fathers and mothers should not marry with their own children, is not that too a general command?"

"No," answered Hippias, "this last law is not a Divine law, because I see some persons trangress it."

"They observe not the others better," said Socrates; "but take notice, that no man violates with impunity a law established by the gods. There are unavoidable punishments annexed to this crime; but we easily secure ourselves from the rigour of human laws, after we have transgressed them, either by keeping ourselves hid, or defending ourselves by open force."

"And what is this punishment," said Hippias, "which it is impossible for fathers, who marry with their own children, to avoid?"

"It is very great," said Socrates; "for what can be more afflicting to men, who desire to have children than to have very bad ones?"

"And how do you know," pursued Hippias, "that they will have bad children? What shall hinder them, if they are virtuous themselves, from having children that are so likewise?"

"It is not enough," answered Socrates, "that the father and the mother be virtuous: they must, besides, be both of them in the vigour and perfection of their age. Now, do you believe, that the seed of persons who are too young, or who are already in their declining age, is equal to that of persons who are in their full strength?"

"It is not likely that it is," said Hippias.

"And which is the best?" pursued Socrates.

"Without doubt," said Hippias, "that of a man in his strength."

"It follows, then," continued Socrates, "that the seed of persons who are not yet come to their full strength, or who are past it, is not good."

"In all appearance it is not."

"In those ages, then, we ought not to get children?" said Socrates.

"I think so."

"Such, therefore, as indulge their lust in such untimely fruition will have very weakly children?"

"I grant they will."

"And are not weakly children bad ones?"

"They are," said Hippias.

"Tell me, further," said Socrates, "is it not an universal law to do good to those who have done good to us?"

"Yes," said Hippias, "but many offend against this law."

"And they are punished for it," replied Socrates, "seeing their best friends abandon them, and that they are obliged to follow those who have an aversion for them. For are not they the best friends who do kindnesses whenever they are desired? And if he who has received a favour neglect to acknowledge it, or return it ill, does he not incur their hate by his ingratitude? And yet, finding his advantage in preserving their goodwill, is it not to them that he makes his court with most assiduity?"

"It is evident," said Hippias, "that it is the gods who have ordered these things; for, when I consider that each law carries with it the punishment of the transgressor, I confess it to be the work of a more excellent legislator than man."

"And do you think," said Socrates, "that the gods make laws that are unjust?"

"On the contrary," answered Hippias, "it is very diffcult for any but the gods to make laws that are just."

"Therefore, Hippias," said Socrates, "according to the gods themselves 'to obey the laws is to be just.'"

This is what Socrates said on the subject of justice, and his actions being conformable to his words, he from day to day created a greater love of justice in the minds of those who frequented him.

CHAPTER V

OF THE MISCHIEFS OF INTEMPERANCE,
AND THE ADVANTAGES OF SOBRIETY

I will now set down the arguments that Socrates used to bring his friends to the practice of good actions, for being of opinion that temperance is a great advantage to such as desire to do anything that is excellent, he first showed them, by his way of living, that no man was more advanced than himself in the exercise of that virtue; and in his conferences he exhorted his hearers above all things to the practice of it, and his thoughts being continually employed in the means of arriving to be virtuous, he made it likewise the subject of all his discourses.

I remember that talking once with Euthydemus concerning temperance he delivered himself to this effect: — "In your opinion, Euthydemus, is liberty a very valuable thing?"

"To be valued above all things," answered Euthydemus.

"Do you believe that a man who is a slave to sensual pleasures, and finds himself incapable of doing good, enjoys his liberty?"

"Not in the least."

"You allow, then, that to do good is to be free, and that to be prevented from doing it, by any obstacle whatever, is not to be free?"

"I think so," said Euthydemus.

"You believe, then," said Socrates, "that debauched persons are not free?"

"I do."

"Do you believe likewise," continued Socrates, "that debauchery does not only hinder from doing good, but compels to do ill?"

"I think it does."

"What would you say, then, of a master who should hinder you from applying yourself to what is honest, and force you to undertake some infamous occupation?"

"I would say he was a very wicked master," answered Euthydemus.

"And which is the worst of all slaveries?" added Socrates.

"To serve ill masters," said Euthydemus.

"Therefore," inferred Socrates, "the debauched are in a miserable slavery."

"No doubt of it."

"Is it not debauchery, likewise," said Socrates, "that deprives men of their wisdom, the noblest gift of the gods, and drives them into ignorance and stupidity, and all manner of disorders? It robs them of leisure to apply themselves to things profitable, while it drowns them in sensual pleasures; and it seizes their minds to that degree that, though they often know which is the best way, they are miserably engaged in the worst."

"They are so."

"Nor can we expect to find temperance nor modesty in a debauched person, since the actions of temperance and debauchery are entirely opposite."

"There is no doubt of it," said Euthydemus.

"I do not think neither," added Socrates, "that it is possible to imagine anything that makes men neglect their duty more than debauchery."

"You say true."

"Is there anything more pernicious to man," said Socrates, "than that which robs him of his judgment, makes him embrace and cherish things that are hurtful, avoid and neglect what is profitable, and lead a life contrary to that of good men?"

"There is nothing," said Euthydemus.

Socrates went on: — "And may we not ascribe the contrary effects to temperance?"

"Without doubt."

"And is it not likely to be true that the cause of the contrary effects is good?"

"Most certainly."

"It follows, then, my dear Euthydemus," said Socrates; "that temperance is a very good thing?"

"Undoubtedly it is."

"But have you reflected," pursued Socrates, "that debauchery, which pretends to lead men to pleasures, cannot conduct them thither, but deceives them, leaving them in disappointment, satiety, and disgust? and have you considered that temperance and sobriety alone give us the true taste of pleasures? For it is the nature of debauchery not to endure hunger nor thirst, nor the fatigue of being long awake, nor the vehement desires of love, which, nevertheless, are the true dispositions to eat and drink with delight, and to find an exquisite pleasure in the soft approaches of sleep, and in the enjoyments of love. This is the reason that the intemperate find less satisfaction in these actions, which are necessary and frequently done. But temperance, which accustoms us to wait for the necessity, is the only thing that makes us feel an extreme pleasure in these occasions."

"You are in the right," said Euthydemus.

"It is this virtue, too," said Socrates, "that puts men in a condition of bringing to a state of perfection both the mind and the body, of rendering themselves capable of well governing their families, of being serviceable to their friends and their country, and of overcoming their enemies, which is not only very agreeable on account of the advantages, but very desirable likewise for the satisfaction that attends it. But the debauched know none of this, for what share can they pretend to in virtuous actions, they whose minds are wholly taken up in the pursuit of present pleasures?"

"According to what you say," replied Euthydemus, "a man given to voluptuousness is unfit for any virtue."

"And what difference is there," said Socrates, "between an irrational animal and a voluptuous man, who has no regard to what is best, but blindly pursues what is most delightful? It belongs to the temperate only to inquire what things are best and what not; and then, after having found out the difference by experience and reasoning, to embrace the good and avoid the bad, which renders them at once most happy, most virtuous, and most prudent."

This was the sum of this conference with Euthydemus. Now Socrates said that conferences were so called because the custom was to meet and confer together, in order to distinguish things according to their different species, and he advised the frequent holding of these conferences, because it is an exercise that improves and makes men truly great, teaches them to become excellent politicians, and ripens the judgment and understanding.

CHAPTER VI

SOCRATES' FRIENDS ATTAIN, BY FREQUENTING HIS CONVERSATION, AN EXCELLENT WAY OF REASONING. — THE METHOD HE OBSERVED IN ARGUING SHOWN IN SEVERAL INSTANCES. — OF THE DIFFERENT SORTS OF GOVERNMENT. — HOW SOCRATES DEFENDED HIS OPINIONS

I will show, in the next place, how Socrates' friends learnt to reason so well by frequenting his conversation. He held that they who perfectly understand the nature of things can explain themselves very well concerning them, but that a man who has not that knowledge often deceives himself and others likewise. He therefore perpetually conferred with his friends without ever being weary of that exercise. It would be very difficult to relate how he defined every particular thing. I will therefore mention only what I think sufficient to show what method he observed in reasoning. And, in the first place, let us see how he argues concerning piety.

"Tell me," said he to Euthydemus, "what piety is?"

"It is a very excellent thing," answered Euthydemus.

"And who is a pious man?" said Socrates.

"A man who serves the gods."

" Is it lawful," added Socrates "to serve the gods in what manner we please?"

"By no means," said Euthydemus; "there are laws made for that purpose, which must be kept."

"He, then, who keeps these laws will know how he ought to serve the gods?"

"I think so."

"And is it not true," continued Socrates, "that he who knows one way of serving the gods believes there is no better a way than his?"

"That is certain."

"And will he not be careful how he does otherwise?"

"I believe he will."

"He, then, who knows the laws that ought to be observed in the service of the gods, will serve them according to the laws?"

"Without doubt."

"But he who serves the gods as the laws direct, serves them as he ought?"

"True, he does."

"And he who serves the gods as he ought is pious?"

"There can be no doubt of it."

"Thus, then," said Socrates, "we have the true definition of a pious man: He who knows in what manner he ought to serve the gods?"

"I think so," said Euthydemus.

"Tell me further," continued Socrates, "is it lawful for men to behave themselves to one another as they please?"

"In nowise," answered Euthydemus; " there are also certain laws which they ought to observe among themselves."

"And do they," said Socrates, "who live together according to those laws, live as they ought?"

"Yes."

"And do they who live as they ought live well?"

"Certainly they do."

"And does he who knows how to live well with men understand well how to govern his affairs?"

"It is likely that he may."

"Now, do you believe," said Socrates, "that some men obey the laws without knowing what the laws command?"

"I do not believe it."

"And when a man knows what he ought to do, do you think he believes that he ought not to do it?"

"I do not think so."

"And do you know any men who do otherwise than they believe they ought to do?"

"None at all."

"They, then, who know the laws that men ought to observe among themselves, do what those laws command?"

"I believe so."

"And do they who do what the laws command, do what is just?"

"Most surely."

"And they who do what is just are just likewise?"

"None but they are so."

"We may, therefore, well conclude," said Socrates, "that the just are they who know the laws that men ought to observe among themselves?"

"I grant it," said Euthydemus.

"And as for wisdom," pursued Socrates, "what shall we say it is? Tell me whether are men said to be wise in regard to the things they know, or in regard to those they do not know?"

"There can be no doubt," answered Euthydemus, "but that it is in consideration of what they know; for how can a man be wise in things he knows not?"

"Then," said Socrates, "men are wise on account of their knowledge?" "It cannot be otherwise."

"Is wisdom anything but what renders us wise?"

"No."

"Wisdom therefore is only knowledge?"

"I think so."

"And do you believe," said Socrates, "that it is in the power of a man to know everything?"

"Not so much as even the hundredth part."

"It is, then, impossible," said Socrates, "to find a man who is wise in all things?"

"Indeed it is," said Euthydemus.

"It follows, then," said Socrates, "that every man is wise in what he knows?"

"I believe so."

"But can we, by this same way of comparison, judge of the nature of good?"

"As how?" said Euthydemus.

"Do you think," said Socrates, "that the same thing is profitable to all men?"

"By no means."

"Do you believe that the same thing may be profitable to one and hurtful to another?"

"I think it may."

"Then is it not the good that is profitable?"

"Yes, certainly."

"Therefore, 'what is profitable is a good to him to whom it is profitable.'"

"That is true."

"Is it not the same with what is beautiful? For, can you say that a body or a vessel is beautiful and proper for all the world?"

"By no means."

"You will say, then, that it is beautiful in regard to the thing for which it is proper?"

"Yes."

"But tell me whether what is reputed beautiful for one thing has the same relation to another as to that to which it is proper?"

"No."

"Then 'whatever is of any use is reputed beautiful in regard to the thing to which that use relates?'"

"I think so."

"And what say you of courage?" added Socrates. "Is it an excellent thing?"

"Very excellent," answered Euthydemus.

"But do you believe it to be of use in occasions of little moment?"

"Yes; but it is necessary in great affairs."

"Do you think it of great advantage in dangers," continued Socrates, "not to perceive the peril we are in?"

"I am not of that opinion."

"At that rate," said Socrates, "they who are not frightened because they see not the danger are in nowise valiant."

"There is no doubt of it," said Euthydemus, "for otherwise there would be some fools, and even cowards, who must be accounted brave."

"And what are they who fear what is not to be feared?"

"They are less brave than the others," answered Euthydemus.

"They therefore," said Socrates, "who show themselves valiant in dangerous occasions, are they whom you call brave; and they who behave themselves in them unworthily, are they whom you call cowards?"

"Very right."

"Do you think," added Socrates, "that any men are valiant in such occasions except they who know how to behave themselves in them?"

"I do not think there are."

"And are not they, who behave themselves unworthily, the same as they who know not how to behave themselves?"

"I believe they are."

"And does not every man behave himself as he believes he ought to do?"

"Without doubt."

"Shall we say, then, that they who behave themselves ill know how they ought to behave themselves?"

"By no means."

"They, therefore, who know how to behave themselves, are they who behave themselves well?"

"They and no others."

"Let us conclude, then," said Socrates, "that they who know how to behave themselves well in dangers and difficult occasions are the brave, and that they who know not how to do so are the cowards."

"That is my opinion," said Euthydemus.

181

Socrates was wont to say, that a kingly government and a tyrannical government were indeed two sorts of monarchy, and that there was this difference between them; that, under a kingly government, the subjects obeyed willingly, and that everything was done according to the laws of the State; but that, under a tyrannical government, the people obeyed by force, and that all the laws were reduced to the sole will of the sovereign.

Concerning the other sorts of government, he said: That when the offices of a Republic are given to the good citizens, this sort of State was called aristocracy, or government of good men; when, on the contrary, the magistrates were chosen according to their revenues, it was called a plutocracy, or government of the rich; and when all the people are admitted, without distinction, to bear employments, it is a democracy, or popular government.

If any one opposed the opinion of Socrates, on any affair whatever, without giving a convincing reason, his custom was to bring back the discourse to the first proposition, and to begin by that to search for the truth. For example: if Socrates had commended any particular person, and any stander-by had named another, and pretended that he was more valiant, or more experienced in affairs, he would have defended his opinion in the following manner:—

"You pretend," would he have said, "that he of whom you speak is a better citizen than the person whom I was praising. Let us consider what is the duty of a good citizen, and what man is most esteemed in a Republic. Will you not grant me, that in relation to the management of the public revenue, he is in the highest esteem who, while he has that office, saves the Republic most money? In regard to the war, it is he who gains most victories over the enemies. If we are to enter into a treaty with other States, it is he who can dexterously win over to the party of the Republic those who before opposed its interests. If we are to have regard to what passes in the assemblies of the people, it is he who breaks the cabals, who appeases the seditious, who maintains concord and unity among the citizens." This being granted him, he applied these general rules to the dispute in question, and made the truth plainly appear, even to the eyes of those who contradicted him. As for himself, when he undertook to discourse of anything, he always began by the most common and universally received propositions, and was wont to say, that the strength of the argumentation consisted in so doing. And, indeed, of all the men I have ever seen, I know none who could so easily bring others to own the truth of what he had a mind to prove to them. And he said that Homer, speaking of Ulysses, called him "the certain or never-failing orator," because he had the art of supporting his arguments upon principles that were acknowledged by all men.

CHAPTER VII

METHOD TO BE OBSERVED IN STUDY. — ARTS AND SCIENCES NO FURTHER USEFUL, THAN THEY CONTRIBUTE TO RENDER MEN WISER, BETTER, OR HAPPIER. — VAIN AND UNPROFITABLE KNOWLEDGE TO BE REJECTED

I presume now, that what I have said has been a sufficient evidence of the frankness and sincerity with which Socrates conversed with his friends, and made known his opinions to them. It remains now that I should say something of the extreme care Socrates showed for the advancement of his friends, and how much he had at heart that they might not be ignorant of anything that could be useful to them, to the end they might not want the assistance of others in their own affairs. For this reason, he applied himself to examine in what each of them was knowing; then, if he thought it in his power to teach them anything that an honest and worthy man ought to know, he taught them such things with incredible readiness and affection; if not, he carried them himself to masters who were able to instruct them. But he resolved within himself how far a person who was well-educated in his studies ought to learn everything.

Thus for geometry he said, that we ought to know enough of it not to be imposed upon in measure when we buy or sell land, when we divide an inheritance into shares, or measure out the work of a labourer, and that it was so easy to know this, that if a man applied himself ever so little to the practice of such things, he would soon learn even the extent and circumference of the whole earth, and how to measure it; but he did not approve that a man should dive into the very bottom of this science, and puzzle his brains with I know not what figures, though he himself was expert in it, for he said he could not see what all those niceties and inventions were good for, which take up the whole life of a man, and distract him from other more necessary studies.

In like manner he was of opinion that a man should employ some time in astronomy, that he might know by the stars the hour of the night, what day of the month it is, and what season of the year we are in, in order that we might know when to relieve a sentinel in the night, and when it is best to venture out to sea, or undertake a journey, and, in short, that we might know how to do everything in its proper season. He said that all this was easily learnt by conversing with seamen, or with such as go a-hunting by night, or others who profess to know these things; but he dissuaded very much from penetrating farther into this science, as even to know what planets are not in the same declination, to explain all their different motions, to know how far distant they are from the earth, in how long time they make their revolutions, and what are their several influences, for he thought these sciences wholly useless, not that he was ignorant of them himself, but because they take up all our time, and divert us from better employments.

In fine, he could not allow of a too curious inquiry into the wonderful workmanship of the Deity in the disposition of the universe, that being a secret which the mind cannot comprehend, and because it is not an action acceptable to God to endeavour to discover what He would hide from us. He held, likewise, that it was dangerous to perplex the mind with these sublime speculations, as Anaxagoras had done, who pretended to be very knowing in them, for in teaching that the sun was the same thing as fire, he does not consider that fire does not dazzle the eyes, but that it is impossible to support the splendour of the sun. He did not reflect, neither, that the sun blackens the sky, which fire does not; nor lastly, that the heat of the sun is necessary to the earth, in order to the production of trees and fruits, but that the heat of fire burns and kills them. When he said, too, that the sun was only a stone set on fire, he did not consider that a stone glitters not in the fire, and cannot last long in it without consuming, whereas the sun lasts always, and is an inexhaustible source of light.

Socrates advised, likewise, to learn arithmetic, but not to amuse ourselves with the vain curiosities of that science, having established this rule in all his studies and in all his conferences, never to go beyond what is useful.

He exhorted his friends to take care of their health, and to that purpose to consult with the learned; and to observe, besides, each in his own particular, what meat, what drink, and what exercise is best for him, and how to use them to preserve himself in health. For when a man has thus studied his own constitution, he cannot have a better physician than himself.

If any one desired to attempt or to learn things that were above the power or capacity of human nature, he advised him to apply himself to divination; for he who knows by what means the gods generally signify their mind to men, or how it is they used to give them counsel and aid, such a person never fails to obtain from the Deity all that direction and assistance that is necessary for him.

CHAPTER VIII

BEHAVIOUR OF SOCRATES FROM THE TIME OF HIS CONDEMNATION TO HIS DEATH. — HIS CHARACTER SUMMED UP IN A FEW WORDS

To conclude: if, because Socrates was condemned to death, any one should believe that he was a liar to say that he had a good demon that guided him, and gave him instructions what he should or should not do, let him consider, in the first place, that he was arrived to such an age that if he had not died when he did, he could not have lived much longer; that by dying when he did he avoided the most toilsome part of life, in which the mind loses much of its vigour; and that in amends for it he discovered to the whole world the greatness of his soul, acquired to himself an immortal glory, by the defence he made before his judges, in behaving himself with a sincerity, courage, and probity that were indeed wonderful, and in receiving his sentence with a patience and resolution of mind never to be equalled; for it is agreed by all that no man ever suffered death with greater constancy than Socrates.

He lived thirty days after his condemnation, because the Delian feasts happened in that month, and the law forbids to put any man to death till the consecrated vessel that is sent to the Isle of Delos be come back to Athens. During that time his friends, who saw him continually, found no change in him; but that he always retained that tranquillity of mind and agreeableness of temper which before had made all the world admire him. Now, certainly no man can die with greater constancy than this; this is doubtless the most glorious death that can be imagined; but if it be the most glorious, it is the most happy; and if it be the most happy, it is the most acceptable to the Deity. Hermogenes has told me, that being with him a little after Melitus had accused him, he observed, that he seemed to decline speaking of that affair: from whence he took occasion to tell him that it would not be amiss for him to think of what he should answer in his own justification. To which Socrates replied: "Do you believe I have done anything else all my life than think of it?" And Hermogenes asking him what he meant by saying so? Socrates told him that he had made it the whole business of his life to examine what was just and what unjust; that he had always cherished justice and hated injustice, and that he did not believe there was any better way to justify himself.

Hermogenes said further to him: — "Do you not know that judges have often condemned the innocent to death, only because their answers offended them, and that, on the contrary, they have often acquitted the guilty?"

"I know it very well," answered Socrates; "but I assure you, that having set myself to think what I should say to my judges, the demon that advises me dissuaded me from it." At which Hermogenes seeming surprised, Socrates said to him, "Why are you surprised that this God thinks it better for me to leave this world than to continue longer in it? Sure, you are not ignorant that I have lived as well and as pleasantly as any man, if to live well be, as I take it, to have no concern but for virtue, and if to live pleasantly be to find that we have made some progress in it. Now, I have good reason to believe that this is my happy case, that I have always had a steady regard for virtue, and made progress in it, because I perceive that my mind, at this time, doth not misgive me; nay, I have the sincere testimony of my conscience that I have done my duty; and in this belief I strengthen myself by the conversation I have had with others, and by comparing myself with them. My friends, too, have believed the same thing of me, not because they wish me well, for in that sense every friend would think as much of his friend, but because they thought they advanced in virtue by my conversation.

"If I were to live longer, perhaps I should fall into the inconveniences of old age: perhaps my sight should grow dim, my hearing fail me, my judgment become weak, and I should have more trouble to learn, more to retain what I had learnt; perhaps, too, after all, I should find myself incapable of doing the good I had done before. And if, to complete my misery, I should have no sense of my wretchedness, would not life be a burden to me? And, on the other hand, say I had a sense of it, would it not afflict me beyond measure? As things now stand, if I die innocent the shame will fall on those who are the cause of my death, since all sort of iniquity is attended with shame. But who will ever blame me because others have not confessed my innocence, nor done me justice? Past experience lets us see that they who suffer injustice, and they who commit it, leave not a like reputation behind them after their death. And thus, if I die on this occasion, I am most certain that posterity will more honour my memory than theirs who condemn me; for it will be said of me, that I never did any wrong, never gave any ill advice to any man; but that I laboured all my life long to excite to virtue those who frequented me."

This was the answer that Socrates gave to Hermogenes, and to several others. In a word, all good men who knew Socrates daily regret his loss to this very hour, reflecting on the advantage and improvement they made in his company.

For my own part, having found him to be the man I have described, that is to say, so pious as to do nothing without the advice of the Deity; so just as never to have in the least injured any man, and to have done very signal services to many; so chaste and temperate as never to have preferred delight and pleasure before modesty and honesty; so prudent as never to have mistaken in the discernment of good and evil, and never to have had need of the advice of others, to form a right judgment of either; moreover, most capable to deliberate and resolve in all sorts of affairs, most capable to examine into men, to reprehend them for their vices, and to excite them to virtue; having, I say, found all these perfections in Socrates, I have always esteemed him the most virtuous and most happy of all men; and if any one be not of my opinion, let him take the pains to compare him with other men, and judge of him afterwards.

SUGGESTED READING

ANDERSON, J. K. *Xenophon.* London: Scribner's Sons, 1974.

CHROUST, A-H. *Socrates Man and Myth: The Two Socratic Apologies of Xenophon.* Notre Dame, Indiana: Notre Dame University Press, 1957.

GRAY, VIVIENNE J. *The Framing of Socrates: The Literary Interpretation of Xenophon's "Memorabilia."* Stuttgart: Steiner, 1998.

GROTE, G. *Plato and the Other Companions of Socrates,* 3 volumes. London: Murray, 1867.

MOMIGLIANO, A. *The Development of Greek Biography.* Cambridge, Mass.: Harvard University Press, 1971.

MONTUORI, M. *Socrates: An Approach.* Amsterdam: Gieben, 1988.

ROBBINS, R. D. C. *Introduction to Xenophon's "The Memorabilia of Socrates."* New York: American Book Co., 1832.

RUDBERG, G. *Sokrates bei Xenophon. Uppsala Universitätis Arsschrift* 2. Uppsala, Sweden, 1939.

STRAUSS, L. *Xenophon's Socrates.* Ithaca: Cornell University Press, 1972.

VANDER WAERDT, P. A. *The Socratic Movement.* Ithaca: Cornell University Press, 1994.

VLASTOS, G. *Socrates: Ironist and Moral Philosopher.* Ithaca: Cornell University Press, 1991.

Look for the following titles, available now from
The Barnes & Noble Library of Essential Reading.

Visit your Barnes & Noble bookstore,
or shop online at www.bn.com/loer

BEST SELLERS

Age of Revolution	Winston Churchill	0-7607-6859-5	$9.95
Autobiography of Benjamin Franklin	Benjamin Franklin	0-7607-6199-X	$6.95
Autobiography of Charles Darwin `	Charles Darwin	0-7607-6908-7	$7.95
Birth of Britain	Winston Churchill	0-7607-6857-9	$9.95
Common Law	Oliver Wendell Holmes, Jr.	0-7607-5498-5	$9.95
Critique of Judgment	Immanuel Kant	0-7607-6202-3	$7.95
Critique of Pure Reason	Immanuel Kant	0-7607-5594-9	$12.95
Democracy in America	Alexis de Tocqueville	0-7607-5230-3	$14.95
Democracy and Education	John Dewey	0-7607-6586-3	$9.95
Discourse on Method	Rene Descartes	0-7607-5602-3	$4.95
Fall of Troy	Quintus of Smyrna	0-7607-6836-6	$6.95
Flatland	Edwin A. Abbott	0-7607-5587-6	$5.95
Great Democracies	Winston Churchill	0-7607-6860-9	$9.95
Guide for the Perplexed	Moses Maimonides	0-7607-5757-7	$12.95
Introduction to Mathematics	Alfred North Whitehead	0-7607-6588-X	$7.95
Island of Dr. Moreau	H. G. Wells	0-7607-5584-1	$4.95
Leviathan	Thomas Hobbes	0-7607-5593-0	$9.95
Lives of the Caesars	Suetonius	0-7607-5758-5	$9.95
Love and Freindship and Other Early Works	Jane Austen	0-7607-6856-0	$6.95

Man Who Was Thursday	G. K. Chesterton	0-7607-6310-0	$5.95
Martian Tales Trilogy	Edgar Rice Burroughs	0-7607-5585-X	$9.95
Meditations	Marcus Aurelius	0-7607-5229-X	$5.95
Montcalm and Wolfe	Francis Parkman	0-7607-6835-8	$12.95
Montessori Method	Maria Montessori	0-7607-4995-7	$7.95
Mysteries of Udolpho	Ann Radcliffe	0-7607-6315-1	$12.95
New World	Winston Churchill	0-7607-6858-7	$9.95
Nicomachean Ethics	Aristotle	0-7607-5236-2	$7.95
Notes on Nursing	Florence Nightingale	0-7607-4994-9	$4.95
On War	Carl von Clausewitz	0-7607-5597-3	$14.95
Outline of History: Volume 1	H. G. Wells	0-7607-5866-2	$12.95
Outline of History: Volume 2	H. G. Wells	0-7607-5867-0	$12.95
Passing of the Armies	Joshua Lawrence Chamberlain	0-7607-6052-7	$7.95
Personal Memoirs	Ulysses S. Grant	0-7607-4990-6	$14.95
Problems of Philosophy	Bertrand Russell	0-7607-5604-X	$5.95
Recollections and Letters	Robert E. Lee	0-7607-5919-7	$9.95
Relativity	Albert Einstein	0-7607-5921-9	$6.95
Tractatus Logico-Philosophicus	Ludwig Wittgenstein	0-7607-5235-4	$5.95
Trial and Death of Socrates	Plato	0-7607-6200-7	$4.95
Up From Slavery	Booker T. Washington	0-7607-5234-6	$6.95
Voyage of the Beagle	Charles Darwin	0-7607-5496-9	$9.95
Wealth of Nations	Adam Smith	0-7607-5761-5	$9.95
What Is Art?	Leo Tolstoy	0-7607-6581-2	$6.95

THE BARNES & NOBLE
LIBRARY OF ESSENTIAL READING

This newly developed series has been established to provide affordable access to books of literary, academic, and historic value—works of both well-known writers and those who deserve to be rediscovered. Selected and introduced by scholars and specialists with an intimate knowledge of the works, these volumes present complete, original texts in a modern, readable typeface—welcoming a new generation of readers to influential and important books of the past. With more than 100 titles already in print and more than 100 forthcoming, the *Library of Essential Reading* offers an unrivaled variety of thought, scholarship, and entertainment. Best of all, these handsome and durable paperbacks are priced to be exceptionally affordable. For a full list of titles, visit www.bn.com/loer.